Ideology and Development
Sun Yat-sen and the
Economic History
of Taiwan

CHINA RESEARCH MONOGRAPH   23

INSTITUTE OF EAST ASIAN STUDIES

UNIVERSITY OF CALIFORNIA • BERKELEY

CENTER FOR CHINESE STUDIES

Ideology and Development

Sun Yat-sen and the Economic History of Taiwan

A. James Gregor

with Maria Hsia Chang
and Andrew B. Zimmerman

Although the Center for Chinese Studies, Institute of East Asian Studies, is responsible for the selection and acceptance of monographs in this series, responsibility for the opinions expressed in them and for the accuracy of statements contained in them rests with their authors.

Contents

Preface

This study attempts to accomplish several things. First of all, it seeks to provide a brief, but accurate, account of the economic history of the Republic of China on Taiwan. The economic growth and industrialization of Taiwan over the past three decades has been extraordinary. Of all developing communities, Taiwan's history of stable growth with equity has been the most notable. The account that follows outlines that singular history.

More than that, the exposition attempts to trace the impact of the thought of Sun Yat-sen on the actual processes of development pursued on Taiwan. For the first time in English, a serious attempt is made to identify the elements of Sun's original economic program that were actually invoked in the course of Taiwan's development. Nothing in English and very little in Chinese attempts such an enterprise.

Finally, Taiwan's experience is considered from a comparative perspective in an effort to target whatever relevance its experience may have for nations undergoing the same process. In this context some space is devoted to contrasting the realities of the growth phenomenon on Taiwan against the claims of "dependency theory"—the suggestion that less developed communities once lodged in international money market (i.e., "capitalist") relations are necessarily condemned to slow growth and pandemic poverty. Furthermore, Taiwan's experience of a high degree of family income equity throughout the stages of rapid economic growth is employed to counter the contention made by many growth theorists that less developed nations must suffer a necessary tradeoff between growth and equity.

Given its ambitious intentions, this study cannot discharge *all* its obligations to *everyone's* satisfaction. Still, the authors hope that enough will have been accomplished to warrant the writing and justify the reading.

In the course of this work, the authors became indebted to many individuals and many institutions. Lowell Dittmer was patient, yet demanding—to the ultimate best interests of the exposition. Thomas Metzger sustained us with his unflagging enthusiasm. Ramon Myers provided insight—and his published works afforded a high level of scholarship that served as a model. Chalmers Johnson, Leo Rose, Hungdah Chiu, John Franklin Copper, and Robert Scalapino all provided inspiration.

The Center for Chinese Studies and the Institute of International Studies of the University of California, Berkeley, provided the library facilities and much of the assistance that made the work possible. The Institute for Sino-Soviet Studies of George Washington University and the Pacific Cultural Foundation afforded invaluable support. To all these colleagues and those institutions we express our gratitude.

A. J. G.
M. H. C.
A. B. Z.

Berkeley
July 1981

I

Sun Yat-sen and the Ideology of Development

The *min-sheng chu-i* (Principle of the People's Livelihood) formulated by Dr. Sun Yat-sen has served as the cornerstone in the economic construction of the Republic of China and it also is the guiding principle of the various economic measures of the Chinese Government. The "economic miracle" that has been achieved in Taiwan during the past two decades or so is attributable to the thorough implementation of the Principle of the People's Livelihood.— Shih Chien-sheng[1]

The economic development of Taiwan has been the object of considerable professional interest for about a generation. At least in part because of Taiwan's intimate relationship with the United States, and the attendant availability of wide-ranging and responsible statistical information, the processes of economic growth on the island have been the focus of attention for almost thirty years. Today, it is generally recognized that what we have witnessed on Taiwan has been as much an "economic miracle" as any in the twentieth century.

While there is little serious dispute about the spectacular economic development of Taiwan, there is little consensus about how that development was accomplished. There is a tendency, however, to conceive the processes of economic growth and industrial development on Taiwan as having been characterized by a singularly "pragmatic" and "nonideological" disposition. However development was accomplished, inherited ideas have been judged to have had but little influence. Although the ruling Kuomintang was committed to the ideology of Sun Yat-sen—and one of the cardinal concerns of that ideology was the economic development and modernization of China—it would seem that most commentators are prepared to suggest that Sun's intellectual legacy did not influence the program that shaped

---

1. Shih Chien-sheng, "The *Min-sheng chu-i* and the Economic Modernization in Taiwan," *China Forum* 4, no. 2 (July 1977): 79.

Taiwan's transformation. Although Sun's ideology was systematically cultivated by the political leadership of Republican China during the interwar years (and continues to constitute a critical part of the modern belief system on Taiwan), most commentators seem convinced that Sun's thoughts have had little substantive impact on the formulation of Kuomintang economic policy on Taiwan. Thus, in some of the most recent volumes devoted to the Taiwanese developmental experience, Sun Yat-sen's ideas receive at best perfunctory mention. All of this strikes one as counterintuitive. One would have imagined that any collection of ideas, given currency for so long, would have worked some influence on planning and policy formation.

That the leadership of the Kuomintang expected Sun's ideas to exercise directive influence on economic policy is evidenced by Article 142 of the Constitution of the Republic of China, which insists that the "national economy shall be based on [Sun Yat-sen's] Principle of People's Livelihood." Moreover, at the commencement of Taiwan's economic development, it was anticipated that the program to be pursued would be that embodied in Sun's min-sheng chu-i—a program that involved the "coordinated development of . . . agriculture, mining, industry, commerce, communications, and irrigation." The program would "accelerate industrialization and increase the national income . . . enabling [the] people to lead a life of abundance and of equal economic opportunities."[2]

It seems clear that the political leadership on Taiwan conceived its economic policies predicated on the programmatic ideas left by Sun Yat-sen. Implicit in such a claim is the conviction that Sun left, as an intellectual legacy, the elements of a realistic plan of economic development. It is precisely this suggestion that is apparently so difficult for many Western analysts to accept. There is now a fairly well entrenched notion that Sun left very little that could serve as a guide to political conduct or economic planning. Some of the earliest Western commentators on Sun's thought originated the notion, maintaining that it offered little that could serve as a programmatic guide. Karl Wittfogel, shortly after Sun's death, argued that Sun had left a "contradictory" ideology that, at best, could provide only a "very imprecise program."[3] M. N. Roy was even less generous. For Roy, "Sun Yat-sen was remarkably sterile in original thought. . . . As a matter of fact, he did not

---

2. In 1952, when the development of Taiwan was contemplated, the Seventh National Convention of the Kuomintang issued a programmatic platform which predicated the policies of the Party on the *San-min chu-i* of Sun Yat-sen. See "Kuomintang Platform Adopted by the Seventh National Convention," in Sun Yat-sen, *Fundamentals of National Reconstruction* (Taipei: Sino-American Publishing, 1953), pp. 257-266, particularly the "Economic Program," pp. 260-262.
3. Karl A. Wittfogel, *Sun Yat-sen: Aufzeichnungen eines chinesischen Revolutionaers* (Berlin: Agis Verlag, n.d.), pp. 66, 118.

think; he only schemed. . . . Therefore, he failed to provide [his] movement with a comprehensive program."[4] At about the same time an anonymous British critic dismissed Sun by alluding to his "kindergarten economics," "economic heresies," "falsifications," and "absurd statements," all of which resulted in a "political hotch-potch" produced by a man of "so mediocre a mentality" that he might better have been abandoned to custodial care than sought after as a "leader and a political prophet."[5]

While characteristically less tendentious than that, the academic literature of the West, produced after the Second World War, has generally not taken Sun's thought seriously. Allusions are regularly made to his "serious deficiencies as a social and political thinker"—deficiencies that could only produce intellectual and programmatic "inconsistencies."[6] Consequently, there is a predisposition not to consider Sun's ideas in assessing the factors that might have influenced the economic development and industrialization of Taiwan.

All of which does not preclude the possibility of an alternative assessment. Paul Linebarger insisted on the significance as well as the consistency of Sun's thought as early as the mid-thirties; more recently, Gottfried-Karl Kindermann has maintained that not only was Sun's thought "perfectly consistent," but that it offered a collection of programmatic goals and attendant strategies that, in fact, did animate the policies of the political leadership on Taiwan.[7]

It is extremely difficult, of course, to resolve such judgmental disagreements by making anything like a universally compelling argument for either one or the other case. As long as social and political theory is couched in ordinary and academic language, what will qualify as a "contradiction" to

4. M. N. Roy, *Revolution and Counterrevolution in China* (Calcutta: Renaissance Publishers, 1946), pp. 256-257.
5. "Saggitarius," *The Strange Apotheosis of Sun Yat-sen* (London: Heath Cranton, 1939), pp. 160, 174.
6. Benjamin Schwartz, "Foreword," to Edward Friedman, *Backward Toward Revolution* (Berkeley and Los Angeles: University of California Press, 1974), p. x; and Chester C. Tan, *Chinese Political Thought in the Twentieth Century* (Garden City, N.J.: Doubleday & Co., 1971), p. 116. Both allude to those judgments that have become commonplace in the Western literature devoted to Sun's thought. An illustrative example of such judgments may be found in Y. C. Wang, *Chinese Intellectuals and the West, 1872-1949* (Chapel Hill, N.C.: University of North Carolina Press, 1966), pp. 338, 354.
7. See Paul M. A. Linebarger, *The Political Doctrines of Sun Yat-sen* (Westport, Conn.: Hyperion Press, 1973); Gottfried-Karl Kindermann, *Konfuzianismus, Sunyatsenismus und chinesischer Kommunismus* (Freiburg im Breisbau: Rombah & Co., 1963).

one intellectual historian will count as a "profundity" to another. Thinkers from the time of the pre-Socratics to the present have been subject to such conflicting assessments. Leopold Schwarzschild, for example, found only a "motley collection" of "contradictory statements" in the thought of Karl Marx, Gordon Leff could allude to Marx's "weaknesses and inconsistencies," Eugen von Boehm-Bawerk could characterize Marx's ideas as a "house of cards," and no less than Benedetto Croce and Karl Popper could refer to the "sterility" of Marx's entire enterprise.[8] Needless to say, any number of equally qualified academicians have tendered opposing judgments concerning Marx's thought. In such circumstances one makes one's case—and each case is as plausible as the evidence of the critic's objective and systematic treatment of the relevant body of thought is convincing.

With respect to the thought of Sun Yat-sen, many of the judgments made by his most uncompromising critics can be shown to be either the product of bias or ignorance, or both. By way of illustration, M. N. Roy could insist that "until very late in his life, social questions did not bother Sun Yat-sen," when all the evidence we have, embodied in his public statements and his writings—supported by convincing contemporary corroboration—indicates that "social questions" always constituted a central concern for Sun. That concern was evident in his first published communication in 1894, became critical as early as 1899, and constituted the essential part of his ideological formulations as early as 1903.[9] Sun's views, in fact, were among the most radical offered as solutions to China's social problems during the first decades of the twentieth century.[10] The best that might be said of judgments like Roy's is that they are the consequence of inadequate scholarship.

In our own time terms like "incoherence" or "superficiality" are employed with considerably more restraint when applied to Sun's thought. That certain themes persisted in Sun's works can now be established with some assurance. That such themes evolved and matured into greater complexity is equally demonstrable. Whether that development reflected "coherence" or "incoherence" involves many subtle judgments that allow considerable room for the free exercise of simple prejudgment and bias. Whatever the case, it is now more and more frequently granted that "Sun related

---

8. See Leopold Schwarzschild, *The Red Prussian: The Life and Legend of Karl Marx* (London: Hamish Hamilton, 1948), p. 366; Gordon Leff, *The Tyranny of Concepts: A Critique of Marxism* (London: Merlin Press, 1961), p. 15; Eugen von Boehm-Bawerk, *Karl Marx and the Close of His System* (New York: Augustus M. Kelley, 1949), p. 118.
9. Roy, *Revolution and Counterrevolution,* p. 253; Martin Bernal, *Chinese Socialism to 1907* (Ithaca, N.Y.: Cornell University Press, 1976), pp. 49-59.
10. Friedman, *Backward Toward Revolution,* p. 204.

himself seriously to the disheartening problems which confronted him," and further, "that some of his ways of relating to those problems were to have relevance for the future."[11]

Here we will examine the relevance of those ideas for the economic development of Taiwan. To that purpose, there is a manner of representing Sun's ideas that, while remaining faithful to them, might render their coherence, seriousness, and contemporary relevance more immediately self-evident. For Sun displayed an abiding preoccupation with the modernization and economic development of his nation. In one sense or another, all of his ideas can be shown to turn on the issue of China's economic modernization—the systematic and self-sustaining expansion of its agricultural and industrial productivity. That his ideas were to be applied to only a fragment of the nation he sought to unify and modernize neither diminishes their relevance nor compromises their coherence. Continental China was his specific concern, but his conception of economic development has a far broader range of potential application. Sun clearly anticipated some of the central preoccupations of the twentieth century, and however much the articulation of his ideas was shaped by time and circumstance, his thought reflects a remarkable contemporary relevance.

As early as 1894, before he was thirty, Sun Yat-sen made his first public statement—a series of proposals addressed to China's delayed economic development. In a reform proposal submitted to Li Hung-chang, the Imperial Grand Secretary of Chihli Province, Sun spoke of the necessity of rapidly modernizing China's economy.[12] He spoke of the elementary necessity of constructing vast systems of transportation and communication—the necessary prerequisites of a modern economy. He spoke of the need to create an appropriate infrastructure that would serve the needs of rapid industrialization and agricultural modernization. He spoke of the introduction of machine production, the necessity for modern educational and financial institutions, and the promulgation of uniform codes of conduct—all to foster the dissemination of scientific knowledge and to further the individual enterprise and initiative requisite to the development of a modern China. He spoke of the need to introduce modern techniques of plant and animal husbandry and water management—the extensive use of chemical fertilizers, scientific agronomy, and machinery—to offset the low yields that acted as disincentives to agricultural production and that contributed to the oppressive poverty of the vast rural areas of retrograde China.

(margin annotation: move from tradtl. society)

---

11. Schwartz in Friedman, ibid., p. x.
12. Sun Yat-sen, "Shang Li Hung-chang ch'en chiu-kuo ta-chi-shu" [Memorial to Li Hung-chang on the plan to save the nation], in _Kuo-fu ch'üän-chi_ [The complete works of Sun Yat-sen], (Taipei: Kuomintang Party History Committee, 1973), 3: 1-11. Hereafter cited as _KFCC._

Sun's first proposals for economic development outlined a prototypic example of a strategy calculated to achieve multiple objectives: agricultural modernization, industrialization, and improved income distribution. It was a strategy not only designed to afford the nation the strength to resist the depredations of the foreign powers that everywhere threatened China's territorial integrity and sovereignty, but one committed to serve "the people's livelihood" (*min-chien yang-sheng*), mitigating the bitter poverty that weighed so heavily on his conationals. This was Sun's first public reference to the "principle of the people's livelihood" that was to remain central to all his subsequent thought.

The concern with the "livelihood of the people" was traditional among Chinese thinkers, and found expression in a variety of forms. It appears regularly in Confucian and neo-Confucian texts. By 1895 Sun used the shorter form, *min-sheng*, to express that same preoccupation in the four-point program of the Hsing-chung hui—the organization that was to serve as the forerunner of the T'ung-meng hui, and the subsequent Kuomintang. Whatever the form, the expression "the people's livelihood," when employed by Sun, came to mean a collection of renovative and developmental programs calculated to increase the productivity of agriculture, develop the transportation and communications infrastructure of the nation, establish modern schools and industries, and introduce codes for the governance of social and political life, finance, and commerce.

The expressions *min-sheng* and *kuo-chi min-sheng* were formulations used by many of Sun's contemporaries to signify a similar collection of programmatic concerns. A min-sheng program would provide for the people, and the people would support a vast program of industrialization and modernization that would make China sufficiently strong and united to resist the threat of dismemberment and colonization. Years later Tai Chi-t'ao was to identify the principle of the people's livelihood as Sun's central preoccupation—a principle whose implementation would bring not only well-being to the masses, but "salvation" to the nation.[13] Min-sheng, in effect, involved the most critical aspirations of Sun Yat-sen.

Although he had already been introduced to Western ideas, Sun Yat-sen put together his first proposals about the modernization and development of China before he knew anything systematic about European and American

---

13. See Key Ray Chong, "Cheung Kuan Ying (1841-1920): A Source of Sun Yat-sen's Nationalist Ideology?" *Journal of Asian Studies* 28, no. 2 (February 1969): 247-267; Tai Chi-t'ao, *Die geistigen Grundlagen des Sun Yat Senismus* (Berlin: Wuerfel Verlag, 1931), p. 11. For the earliest employments of the term "min-sheng," see Sun Tzu-ho, "The Political Program of the Hsing-chung hui," *China Forum* 3, no. 2 (July 1976): 133-166.

social and economic thought. He employed the term min-sheng to refer to those ideas, and min-sheng was to occupy the critical center of the final doctrinal statement of his views in the *San-min chu-i,* delivered shortly before his death in 1925.

Between 1894 and 1925, of course, the doctrine of min-sheng became increasingly complex and sophisticated. Nevertheless, its central themes were to remain remarkably constant. A concern for the livelihood of the people entailed a commitment to the agricultural and industrial development of China in order to provide for its independence and sovereignty in the face of multiple external threats. Thus, neither a concern with the "social question" nor a preoccupation with "imperialism" was late in occupying Sun. As early as 1894 he conceived both subject to resolution if only China could be rapidly modernized and industrialized—a conviction he never abandoned.

By 1895 Sun no longer believed that China's development might be accomplished through political reform of the Manchu government. He became an advocate of the revolutionary overthrow of Imperial rule. But whatever his convictions concerning the instrumental roles of reform or revolution, he continued to address himself to the same problems with which he had grappled in his reform petition to Li Hung-chang. Thus in 1897, even after he had given himself over to political revolution and had been recognized as a dangerous revolutionary by the government, Sun continued to identify the two critical problems that faced China as its "apparent inability . . . to develop [its] vast internal resources and [its inability] to resist external attack."[14] These were the same problems that had prompted his reform petition three years earlier. By 1897 he had become convinced that the universal and systematic corruption that attended the rule of the Manchu dynasty was largely responsible for China's developmental incapacities and defensive weaknesses. He called for the overthrow of the "foreign monarchy" and the introduction of some "form of representative government."[15]

By 1897, therefore, Sun had already expressed the three themes that were to give substance to his ideology: a rededication of Chinese nationalism, the establishment of representative government, and his own form of socialism. At thirty, Sun had put together the outlines of his political program. At its center was the min-sheng, his doctrine of Chinese socialism.

That Sun Yat-sen identified this doctrine with a broadly conceived socialism as early as 1896 or 1897 is now reasonably well established.[16] There

---

14. Sun, "China's Present and Future: The Reform Party's Plea for British Benevolent Neutrality," *KFCC* 5: 81.
15. Sun, "Kidnapped in London," ibid., p. 11.
16. Harold Z. Schiffrin, *Sun Yat-sen and the Origins of the Chinese Revolution* (Berkeley and Los Angeles: University of California Press, 1968), pp. 116-117.

is evidence, for example, that Sun was aware of the discussions of Western socialism that had begun to appear in Chinese publications as early as 1890. But the socialism that was the object of Chinese interest had very little to do with anything that might pass as Marxist "orthodoxy." Most of the material that appeared in China at that time concerned itself with the socialisms that were popular in the West at the end of the nineteenth century. In 1891, for example, the influential *Review of the Times*—published by Christian missionaries—provided a serial translation of Edward Bellamy's *Looking Backward,* a novel that heralded a socialistic future world without international strife, capitalist cupidity, or imperialist oppression. The future, for Bellamy, would be characterized by an advanced, collectivistic, industrial system that would provide abundantly, and equitably, for all.[17] We know that Sun was familiar with the *Review of the Times* from about 1889 onwards and probably read the serialization of Bellamy's novel in its pages.

Many Chinese intellectuals of the period saw in Bellamy's social criticism a reflection of the moral and social concerns of traditional Confucianism. By the time Bellamy's book appeared, a number of Chinese scholars had attempted to give Confucianism a contemporary reference. K'ang Yu-wei and Liang Ch'i-ch'ao, who were to serve as the nation's principal intellectual leaders during the reform period before the end of the century, had put together an interpretation of Confucianism that conceived the reflections of the Chinese sage as a guide to the future, rather than simply a historical record of traditional ethical injunctions.

K'ang Yu-wei, who had earlier undertaken a "higher criticism" of the traditional Confucian texts, by 1885 had composed the first draft of *Ta-t'ung shu*—an account of a future world animated by Confucian virtues. After Bellamy's book appeared in Chinese translation, K'ang's conceptions of that future Confucian world began to take on the features of a universal society made abundant by advanced industrial technology and rendered humane by the influence of traditional Chinese social and political virtues. K'ang's ideas began to resemble the kind of socialism to be found in the works of Bellamy and of Henry George. In the final version of his *Ta-t'ung shu,* K'ang's views could only be described as a form of non-Marxist, Chinese socialism.[18] It is clear that Liang Ch'i-ch'ao had given K'ang's ideas considerable circulation during the period when Sun was closest to the major gentry reformers of Imperial China.

---

17. Li Yu-ning, *The Introduction of Socialism into China* (New York: Columbia University Press, 1971), p. 3; the serialization of Bellamy's book appeared in the *Review of the Times,* issues 35-49, December 1891-April 1892.
18. See K'ang Yu-wei, *Ta-t'ung shu,* trans. Laurence G. Thompson (London: George Allen & Unwin, 1958).

Sun was attracted by that kind of socialism, current in the China of his day. This developmental socialism, predicated on technological and industrial advance, shared complex affinities with the intellectual and moral traditions of China. It sought the renovation, rehabilitation, and international security of the nation. It was predicated as much on selected traditional, as on Western, ideas. The Chinese components probably derived from K'ang, and their influence surfaced regularly in Sun's thought.

K'ang, like most of the advanced Chinese thinkers of his time, conceived the world progressing through evolutionary stages. For K'ang those stages involved the transition from an Age of Disorder (*chü-luan shih*), through an Age of Approaching Peace (*sheng-p'ing shih*), to an ultimate Age of Universal Peace (*t'ai-p'ing shih*), or Great Harmony (*ta-t'ung*). K'ang understood each age as having a particular political form and as suffering particular attendant hazards. He saw his age as one of transition, moving from rule by absolute, to rule by constitutional, monarchs. It was an age in which efforts would be made to establish constitutional rule and in which nations would contend with nations. Only at the conclusion of the age then emerging, the Age of Approaching Peace, could the world expect the final Great Harmony—that age of perfect humanity and an equitable social order.[19] It would be an age of democracy and international peace, an age that cherished the sanctity of labor and provided for public welfare through the social ownership of property.[20]

These were the ideas with which Sun was most probably familiar when he identified himself with the broad current of socialism in 1897. It was a form of socialism composed of traditional Chinese ethical principles, animated by a preoccupation with the hazards and potentials of the Age of Approaching Peace.[21] Like K'ang and many of his contemporaries, both Chinese and Western, Sun conceived the world involved in a protracted evolutionary, and progressive, historic process; for him, as it would for K'ang, the process would conclude with the realization of the goals of the "*min-sheng* principle"—which Sun identified with "Confucius' hope of a 'great commonwealth'."[22]

---

19. See Hao Chang, *Liang Ch'i-ch'ao and Intellectual Transition in China, 1890-1907* (Cambridge: Harvard University Press, 1971), chap. 2.
20. Liang Ch'i-ch'ao, *Intellectual Trends in the Ch'ing Period,* trans. Immanuel C. Y. Hsü (Cambridge: Harvard University Press, 1959), p. 96.
21. For the modified Confucian elements to be found in Sun's political ideology, see A. James Gregor, "Confucianism and the Political Thought of Sun Yat-sen," *Philosophy East and West* 31, no. 1 (January 1981): 55-70.
22. Sun, *San-min chu-i* (Taipei: China Publishing, n.d.), p. 184. Hereafter cited as *SMCI.*

Until that time of fulfillment, however, mankind would remain embroiled in the age of approaching peace. For Sun the three economic problems tormenting that age required a comprehensive land policy, an effective developmental program, and a strategy to deal with the threats mounted by foreign imperialism. By 1897 Sun had already settled on the elements of those policies. In his pursuit of solutions he had probably already become familiar with the work of Henry George. In December 1894 the *Review of the Times* had devoted its pages to a discussion of "land nationalization" and the "single tax," themes that George had made popular in his *Progress and Poverty,* a book that first appeared in a regular American edition in 1880. While in Japan in 1897, Sun read George's work in its entirety for the first time.[23]

In *Progress and Poverty* George argued that the people of China suffered privation and the economy stagnated because throughout the nation "insecurity prevails, production goes on under the greatest disadvantages, and exchange is closely fettered. Where the government," George went on, "is a succession of squeezings, and security for capital of any sort must be purchased of a mandarin, [millions will find themselves] . . . just on the verge of starvation."[24] It was not excess population nor the dearth of arable land that produced the calamitous and retrograde conditions of China, but a constellation of political and social constraints on indigenous production and distribution. George went on to address himself to the problem of oppressive rackrents that agrarian tenants were compelled to pay in various parts of the world—rents that served as grievous disincentives to agricultural development and efficiency.[25]

In his essay "China's Present and Future," published in 1897,[26] Sun expanded upon these assessments. China's agrarian problems were not the consequence of overpopulation or of the insufficiency of arable land. The fact that foodstuffs could not be transported from areas of agricultural abundance to those suffering harvest failures without passing through an inordinate number of local impost stations, for example, caused local famine and deterred farmers in fertile areas from growing larger crops. Vast areas remained fallow as a consequence. Foreigners had further complicated China's agrarian problems by imposing "free trade" requirements on the nation—allowing foodstuffs to enter China without import duties, thereby underselling local products to the detriment of local production. The

---

23. See Marius B. Jansen, *The Japanese and Sun Yat-sen* (Stanford, Calif.: Stanford University Press, 1954).
24. Henry George, *Progress and Poverty* (New York: Schalkenbach Publishers, 1953), pp. 121-122.
25. Ibid., pp. 124-125.
26. Sun, "China's Present and Future," *KFCC* 5: 81-109.

consequence was not only the decline of agricultural productivity and the abandonment of marginal but arable land, but a dearth of indigenously generated investment capital as well.

In his discussion with Liang Ch'i-ch'ao and Chang Ping-lin in 1899, Sun elaborated on his concerns. Chinese agriculture had remained inadequate both to feed the nation and as a base for economic development not only because of the corruption of mandarin officials, impaired transportation facilities, and competition with "imperialist" trade, but because tenant farmers were compelled to pay "half of what they produce to the landlords." In Sun's judgment a more equitable arrangement would render the peasants prosperous and release capital for self-sustaining national development. The best solution, he argued at that time, would be that "all who can till should receive land."[27]

After 1903, and particularly after the founding of the T'ung-meng hui in the summer of 1905, Sun's land policies became the focus of critical attention. In their oath to the revolution, Sun's followers swore to uphold what were to become the critical components of the "three principles of the people": the national revival of China, the establishment of political democracy, and what was then called "the equalization of land rights."[28]

The equalization of land rights as Sun and his followers understood it was essentially a gradual application of Henry George's notions concerning a tax on all "unearned increment" that would accrue to land as a consequence of social progress. "Equalization of land rights," as an expression, had appeared in the oath of a branch of Sun's earlier revolutionary organization, the Hsing-chung hui, in Hanoi in 1902. The same expression appeared in the oath of the Revolutionary Military Academy that Sun founded in Japan in 1903 and in the oath that attended the reorganization of one of Sun's groups in San Francisco in 1904. What the expression meant to Sun and his followers became reasonably clear in the exchanges that followed between the authors of Sun's *Min pao* and those of the constitutional monarchists collected around the *Hsin-min ts'ung-pao* of Liang Ch'i-ch'ao (by then intransigently opposed to popular revolution against the Manchu monarchy).

27. As reported in Liang Ch'i-ch'ao, "She-hui ko-ming kuo wei chin-jih Chung-kuo so pi-yao hu," *Hsin-min ts'ung-pao* 86 (December 1906): 32; see also Schiffrin, *Sun Yat-sen,* pp. 308-309.

28. Hu Han-min, "Min pao chih liu ta chu-i" [The six great principles of the *Min pao*], *Min pao* 3 (April 5, 1906): 1-22. The entire collection of the *Min pao,* published between 1905 and 1908, has been republished as *Min pao* (Peking: K'u-hseuh ch'u-pan-she ying-yin, 1957). See also Sun Tzu-ho, "The Political Programs of the T'ung-meng hui," *China Forum* 5, no. 1 (January 1978): 107-108.

In April 1906 and March 1907 Hu Han-min, one of the principal spokesmen for Sun's T'ung-meng hui, provided an exposition of the concept of "equalization of land rights."[29] By equalization of land rights Sun and his followers meant governmental appropriation of "unearned increments" in value rather than the formal abrogation of private land holdings. After the revolution they anticipated, the government would impose a tax on any increments in land value, other than capital improvements, that would take place. Such increments, they argued, would be the consequence of collective social progress and would be returned to the collectivity to fuel the country's industrialization.[30] The policy of equalization of land rights, in and of itself, was not a program of land redistribution. Sun's collaborators conceived it (as Sun consistently conceived it thereafter) as one way to transfer capital from the traditional to the modern sectors of the economy.[31] The agricultural sector was of particular interest as a source of capital accumulation during the early stages of economic development. It was understood that intersectoral capital flows, originating in the traditional sectors of the economy, would ultimately fuel the rapid growth of the modern sectors. Governmental acquisition of the "unearned increment" resulting from the rise in land values that accompanied modernization would provide the capital for self-sustaining growth of the national economy. Such a program would not only preclude the concentration of wealth characteristic of the West; it would free inert capital, otherwise locked into land speculation, for employment in the more dynamic sectors of the economy.

The equalization of land rights clearly meant at least that much, but it was equally evident that it meant something more. Hu went on to include elements of the same convictions concerning land policy that Sun had articulated as early as 1899. Hu, for example, recognized that agricultural tenant labor in China was "oppressed and impoverished" by the land-holding "capitalists." Moreover, because farm laborers were unable to own the lands they tilled, the profits they produced accrued exclusively to the landlords—and

29. Hu, "Min pao" and "Kao fei-nan min-sheng chu-i che" [To the detractors of the Min-sheng chu-i], *Min pao* 12 (March 6, 1907): 45-111.

30. See Robert Scalapino and Harold Z. Schiffrin, "Early Socialist Currents in the Chinese Revolutionary Movement," *Journal of Asian Studies* 18 (May 1959): 332.

31. Hu, "Min pao," p. 13. Years later, Sun expressed the same conviction in the following manner: "When land rights have been equalized, capitalists will be disposed to abandon land speculation and invest in machine enterprise [*chi-yeh*] thus engaging in industry and commerce. Economic development could be the only consequence, since land is limited, while the profits from industry and commerce are potentially limitless." Sun, "Min-sheng chu-i chih shih-shih" [The enactment of the principle of people's livelihood], speech of May 4, 1912, in *KFCC* 2: 232. See also Harold Z. Schiffrin, "Sun Yat-sen's Early Land Policy," *Journal of Asian Studies* 16 (August 1957): 549-564.

capital was thus denied the nation. Only institutionalizing greater equity in the countryside could offset the dysfunctional "dictatorship of the landlords" and apply the profits produced in the agrarian sector to the "benefit of the nation's economy." The application of such policies would produce a "national socialism" (*kuo-yu chu-i*).[32] In effect, although "equalization of land rights" may have, in and of itself, referred only to the collective acquisition of unearned increments on land, the ideologues of the T'ung-meng hui anticipated more extreme rearrangements of property relations in the agrarian sector—rearrangements that would allow not only greater equity, but, at least potentially, land to the tillers as well—all in the service of increasing capital flow from the agricultural to the modern, industrial sector.

Furthermore, while the equalization of land rights constituted the main principle of the min-sheng chu-i for the ideologues of the *Min pao,* such equalization did not exhaust its substance. When Feng Tzu-yu addressed these issues, he identified the political and economic principles of the T'ung-meng hui with "socialism" or "state socialism" (*kuo-chia min-sheng chu-i*)—a program he likened to that of the German government under Bismarck and to that of the post-Meiji Reformation government of Japan. Such programs were better characterized by the interventions of a tutelary state in the national economy than by any preoccupation with state acquisition of unearned increment of land. Such a socialism involved government monopolies of public utilities and special sectors of the economy, a general concern with industrial growth, the "control of capital," and the provision of innovative social welfare programs.[33]

Thus, by 1906 Sun and his theoreticians had put together an ideology of national development comprising a system of land reform, proposals for the indigenous generation of capital, and a rationale for state intervention in the economy. A concern for the "oppressed" agrarian classes was evident, and there was more than a suggestion that Sun's commitment to a program of "land to the tillers" had influenced his followers. These latter concerns were muted, for considerable support was expected from land-holding segments of the population. The T'ung-meng hui was attempting to recruit rather than alienate support. But those concerns remained in evidence

32. Hu, "Min pao," p. 13. Sun continued to refer to his political ideal as a "national socialism." He maintained that "the principle of people's livelihood is the principle of national socialism." Sun, "T'i-ch'ang min-sheng chu-i chih chen-i" [Promote the true meaning of the principle of the people's livelihood], *KFCC* 2: 22.
33. Feng Tzu-yu, "Lu Chung-kuo Jih-pao min-sheng chu-i ho chung-kuo cheng-chih ko-ming chih ch'ien-t'u" [A revised 'Min-sheng chu-i and the future of China's political revolution'], *Min pao* 4 (May 1, 1906): 113. Years later Sun repeated this characterization of the meaning of *min-sheng chu-i*. Sun, "T'i-ch'ang kuo-chia she-hui chu-i" [Promote national socialism], *KFCC* 2: 261.

nonetheless. They were to continue to influence the ideological development of the revolutionaries that collected around Sun until the belief system of the Kuomintang was fully articulated two decades later.

Thus, while all of Sun's followers effusively defended a land tax on unearned increment, they clearly did not imagine that such a tax exhausted either the revolutionary program of the T'ung-meng hui or its land policies. Sun's program was a complex collection of policies for land reform and economic development clearly designed to provide China with at least part of the capital resources that would permit it rapidly to outstrip the West in industrialization, economic development, and defense capabilities.[34]

There was an awareness that indigenously generated capital could not satisfy the capital demands of a developing China. Thus in March 1907 Hu Han-min insisted that while the future revolutionary government's appropriation of value increments on land would provide some of the capital "necessary for [China's] development," the capital resources of the nation were not sufficient to underwrite the complex process of self-sustaining growth. Hu recommended, therefore, that China welcome foreign investment. The United States and Australia, he argued, in pursuing such a policy had become capital-exporting countries. Hu anticipated a similar consequence for China. Hu, in effect, refused to conceive involvement in international trade and investment in terms of a zero-sum game. In commerce and investment it was not necessary for one partner to win at the expense of the other. Foreign investment would certainly return to investors profits that might well be repatriated, but investment generated wages and development and left a concrete legacy in fixed assets in the host country.[35] For the intellectuals of the T'ung-meng hui, and for Sun himself, China's rapid modernization depended on investment capital generated by a tax on "unearned increments," intersectoral capital transfers, and access to the surplus capital markets provided by the advanced industrial countries.

During this entire period, Sun remained concerned with the threat of foreign oppression as well as with China's significant lack of economic modernization and industrial development.[36] Like his collaborators on the staff of *Min pao*, Sun was prepared to acknowledge the threats posed by imperialism—just as he had recognized those threats in his reform letter to Li Hung-chang in 1894 and just as he had done in his support of Filipino revolutionaries in their resistance to American control of their homeland in

---

34. Feng, "Lu Chung-kuo," pp. 97-122.
35. Hu, "Kao fei-nan," pp. 70, 75, 80. This was to represent Sun's views throughout the remainder of his life. See Sun, "Cheng-chien chih piao-shih" [The expression of political opinion], *KFCC* 2: 302-305.
36. Sun, "The True Solution of the Chinese Question," *KFCC* 5: 111-119, 121.

1898.[37] Sun shared with the people around him the notions of imperialism that had become commonplace by the turn of the century. He knew that many of his conationals feared the impact of foreign investment in China. He also knew that impoverished China could not generate the capital necessary for its own self-sustaining growth and modernization. Sun was compelled to formulate a policy concerning relations with the more advanced European nations that would allow China access to international capital resources without compromising China's political independence and sovereignty. What resulted was an interpretation of international relations that distinguished between a program of international economic symbiosis and political and military exploitation.

Sun, like Hu, believed that international trade and financial relations were not intrinsically exploitative. Only when the inflow of foreign capital and the introduction of trade and commerce were attended by military and political interference did international economic relations take on the characteristics of a zero-sum game in which the benefits to one of the participants fell below what could be obtained if those relations were alternatively organized. In such a situation the "exploitation loss" of one participant would constitute the "exploitation gain" of the other. But such relationships could be maintained only if the one participant was politically and militarily so deficient that the maintenance costs of the relationship would not offset any exploitation gains made by the privileged participant. If, on the other hand, the maintenance costs could be made prohibitive, the relationship between participants would be transformed into a "nonzero-sum," or "general," game, in which all could be expected, realistically, to gain.

Throughout his life Sun maintained that international economic relations were not, in and of themselves, exploitative. He argued that in his "age of little peace" international actors would naturally try to maximize their advantages. Where any one participant was demonstrably weak, others could be expected to exploit the opportunity to increase their gains. In numerous instances Sun dolefully recited the economic exploitation of Asians by powerful Western powers. The British in India and the French in Indochina had wrung enormous benefits from their defenseless dependencies. As long as nations are "strong enough to carry out acts of injustice" at minimal costs, he argued, one could hardly expect "respect for justice."[38] As a consequence Sun gave priority to the development of China's defensive capabilities, in order to create an environment in which there would be no

37. Jansen, *The Japanese and Sun Yat-sen,* pp. 68-74.
38. Sun, *The Vital Problem of China* (Taipei: China Cultural Service, 1953), pp. 8-10. This collection, while attributed to Sun, was probably compiled by Chu Chih-hsin. It does, however, represent Sun's views. See C. Martin Wilbur, *Sun Yat-sen: Frustrated Patriot* (New York: Columbia University Press, 1976), pp. 92, 387.

opportunity for exploitation gains without corresponding maintenance costs. Without that capacity China would be dominated by foreign interests and might well remain forever in a "state of serfdom, so that a profitable trade [could] be carried on forever by the ruling country and . . . [China would] always be a market for [their] industrial products."[39]

As long as China remained defenseless, foreign economic exploitation would be the consequence of foreign political and military hegemony. In effect, Sun entertained a *political* conception of exploitative imperialism. He clearly understood that "of the . . . forces [that determine a nation's future] the most potent are political forces and economic forces," and while economic oppression was more severe than political oppression, the former could not be sustained without the prevalence of the latter. For Sun, "imperialism" was the "policy of aggression upon other countries *by means of political force.*" In pursuing security and advantage the "strong states" impose their will on "smaller and weaker peoples."[40] Without effective political and military control of subject peoples, exploitative relations could not be maintained.

Sun's convictions about imperialism clearly differ from the views of classical Marxism and the neo-Marxism of contemporary "dependency theorists." Rather than conceiving imperialism as a necessary product of international trade and financial relations, Sun emphasized considerations of politics, power, and national security in his explanation of exploitative relations between nations. In his judgment, the advantages enjoyed by dominant nations were the consequence of political and military power, and not the result of some inherent necessities of the commercial and financial dynamics of capitalism.[41] Exploitative economic imperialism was, in Sun's judgment, the perfectly rational strategy of foreign policy in a competitive world, in situations of predominant political and military advantage. At the same time he understood that a developing China would require expertise, technology, and capital transfers from those powers most likely to enjoy predominant advantage. In such circumstances China required a deterrent defensive capability; lacking that, the nation would be compelled to form political alliances with those powers with which it shared international and strategic interests.[42] Either would reduce the threat of exploitation.

---

39. Wilbur, ibid., p. 96.
40. Sun, *SMCI,* pp. 8, 10, 21, 23. Emphasis supplied.
41. In this regard, see Hsu Yu-chu, "The Regulation of Private Capital and Equalization of Wealth and Income," *China Forum* 3, no. 2 (July 1976): 69; and the discussion in Benjamin J. Cohen, *The Question of Imperialism* (New York: Basic Books, 1973), pp. 231-245.
42. Sun, *The Vital Problem,* pp. 124-125.

Sun realized that making exploitation expensive would require either the rapid mobilization of the entire armed nation[43] or entry into a system of alliances that would insulate China from the most immediate threats to its sovereignty and security. If either or both could be accomplished, dependency relations could be transformed into relations of interdependency, and exploitative relationships translated into those that would be of mutual advantage. China could then "compete freely with [other nations] in the economic field and be able to hold her own without failure."[44] Political equality would make economic exploitation impossible. In such circumstances, China could "open her markets for the benefit" of international commerce, and welcome "foreign capital to develop . . . industry . . . communication and transportation facilities, and foreign brains and experience to manage them."[45]

Such was Sun's life-long assessment of "imperialism." Unlike contemporary dependency theorists, Sun saw no inevitability of "underdevelopment" for China as a consequence of involvement in the international market economy. In his earliest writings, while deploring imperialism, Sun assiduously sought commercial connections, investment and technology transfers, and the assistance of foreign experts.[46] In 1904, fully cognizant of the threats mounted by imperialism, he nonetheless spoke of his nation as providing "a grand field hitherto never dreamed of . . . to the social and economic activities of the civilized world."[47] In 1918-1919, employing his distinction between economic relations and imperialism, Sun addressed himself to a program for the development of China. He spoke of welcoming foreign trade and capital to help in that development as long as it could be organized to "ensure the mutual benefit of China and of the countries cooperating with us." Possessed of political equality, China would develop in a manner that would ensure the well-being of its citizens, its political integrity, and its international sovereignty, as well as provide a "new market . . . big enough for her own products and for products from foreign countries. . . . The nations," he went on, "which will take part in this development will reap immense advantages. . . . In [such an] undertaking, foreign capital must be invited, foreign experts and organizers have to be enlisted, and gigantic methods have to be adopted. . . . During the construction and the operation of each of these national undertakings, before its capital and

43. Ibid., pp. 126, 128-129.
44. Sun, *SMCI,* p. 208.
45. Sun, *The Vital Problem,* p. 135; *SMCI,* pp. 182-183; and "The Chinese Republic," *The Independent* (New York), September 9, 1912, reproduced in *China Forum* 4, no. 2 (July 1977): 341-342.
46. Sun, "China's Present and Future," *KFCC* 5: 82, 108-109.
47. Sun, "The True Solution," *KFCC* 5: 121.

interest are fully repaid, it will be managed and supervised by foreign experts under Chinese employment. As one of their obligations, these foreign experts have to undertake the training of Chinese assistants to take their place in the future."[48]

The abrogation of unequal treaties as well as the abolition of extraterritoriality and its attendant privileges would allow China the diplomatic and political equality without which exploitation had arisen. Once possessed of such equality, China could invite foreign capital and foreign trade and could expect mutual benefit.

By the time Sun Yat-sen prepared to deliver his lectures on the *San-min chu-i* in 1924, he had put all these elements together to produce a program for economic development as coherent and consistent as any provided by a revolutionary in the twentieth century. The conviction that the motive force of history was the search for, and the maintenance and enhancement of, a way to sustain the livelihood of peoples remained the linchpin of his program throughout his life.[49] To ensure the maintenance and foster the growth of their means of livelihood, communities characteristically harmonize their immediate and conflicting interests within their own boundaries. In the modern world, that harmony finds expression in social legislation, increasing collective control over the means of production, direct taxation to redistribute society's wealth more equitably, and the introduction of cooperative and governmental agencies to distribute commodities more efficiently. When producers and workers collaborate in deciding such policies, the reconciliation of interests ensures social and productive progress that profits all. "Society progresses," Sun maintained, "through the adjustment of major economic interests [rather] than through the clash of interests. [When] the economic interests of society can be harmonized, the majority of people will benefit and society will progress."[50] Believing that all men—capitalists, artisans, merchants, landowners, financiers, as well as industrial and agrarian workers—contribute to that collective enterprise designed to sustain and enhance the livelihood of citizens, Sun rejected the Marxian conception of class warfare as the motive force of historical change. The episodes of social strife and class conflict to which Marx alluded, in Sun's judgment, were instances of "social pathology" rather than evidences of the endemic traits of any social system. Class warfare was evidence of a "diseased" social order. Only in a community that could not provide adequately for its

---

48. Sun, *The International Development of China, KFCC* 5: 129, 130, 132, 135. In 1912 Sun called upon international cooperation in the development of China. See "A Statement and an Appeal by Sun Yat-sen," in James Cantlie, *Sun Yat-sen and the Awakening of China* (London: Fleming H. Revell, 1912), pp. 247-248.
49. Sun, *SMCI*, pp. 155-156.
50. Ibid., pp. 160-161.

members would the functionally and organically related components come into conflict.

To preclude the onset of such disorder, a rational community will provide for the well-being of *all* its members. China, long tormented by the systematic corruption of Manchu rule and the deceitful relations of foreign powers was, in Sun's judgment, threatened with the onset of that kind of pathological disharmony so graphically portrayed in the socialist works prevalent in the West. To prevent the advent of "class warfare," China required an economic program that would provide for the immediate, and enhance the future, well-being of all its citizens.

For Sun, such a program involved "equalization of landownership" and the "regulation of capital." Both were implicit, and often explicit, as early as the exchanges in the *Min pao* of 1906.[51] In 1924 "equalization of landownership" was advanced as precaution against speculation in land, the nonproductive dissipation of scarce capital, and the development of conditions that might foster fratricidal class warfare. Sun proposed a clear determination of the value of land before the rapid development of industry and commerce could inflate it, producing all the disabilities he anticipated. Once the value of land was fixed, all "unearned increments"—increments in value that were not the direct result of capital improvements by the landowner himself— would be taxed. Ownership would remain with the current owner, but the government would reserve the right of purchase at the fixed value in order to serve the public interest.[52] Beyond that, Sun advocated government regulations to protect the peasantry and increase their productivity. He spoke of the oppressive rents that depressed the yield of the working peasantry. He spoke of rents that approximated those of rack-rents, and advocated relief. Finally, Sun spoke of providing "land to the tillers."

Sun had alluded to rent reduction and to providing land to those who actually tilled it as early as 1899. In 1912 he reiterated, "China is an agricultural country. Without solving the basic problems of the peasants, no thorough reforms can be possible. In order to solve the agrarian problem, farmers must own their own lands."[53] In the interim, the discussions in the *Min pao* had been given currency. Finally, in 1924 Sun spelled out his entire agrarian program. The Kuomintang, in his judgment, was compelled by circumstance and simple justice to mobilize peasant support for the revolution.

---

51. Government control of public utilities and monopolies was advocated by both Hu Han-min in his "Kao fei-nan" and by Feng Tzu-yu in his "Lu Chung-kuo," p. 109. Sun collaborated with both authors during this period, and there is little doubt that such views would not have appeared had Sun objected to them.

52. Sun, *SMCI,* pp. 178-179.

53. As cited, Hsueh Chun-tu, *Huang Hsing and the Chinese Revolution* (Stanford, Calif.: Stanford University Press, 1961), p. 141.

To accomplish that, the revolution must appeal to the self-interest of the agrarian working masses. But more than that, a policy of rent reduction and land to the tillers would not only stimulate farm production but would allow critically important revenues, hitherto collected by landlords, to accrue to the state (*kuo-chia*)—a state that would be responsible for implementing a comprehensive agricultural program of scientific agronomy, infrastructural development, water conservancy, and rural irrigation.[54]

As an astute political leader, Sun was often circumspect in addressing his audiences. He did not always and everywhere give equal emphasis to every aspect of his land policy. But there is little doubt that Sun entertained a collection of programmatic ideas concerning a revolutionary land policy for China that included not only a tax on the unearned increment of land but also significant rent relief through legislation, and a correlative but independent policy of providing land to the peasantry. As adjuncts to those ideas, Sun advocated extensive and intensive development of agriculture, not only drawing marginal and uncultivated land into production but also increasing yield by employing machinery, chemical fertilizers, scientific crop rotation, pest control, more effective irrigation, and water conservancy and flood control measures. All of these entailed the collateral development of appropriate educational facilities, machine production, hydro- and thermoelectric power generation, and a mass communications and transportation infrastructure.

Such an ambitious program of development required the intervention of the state through coordinating and controlling agencies; such intervention had all the attributes of the "state socialism" to which the intellectuals of the T'ung-meng hui had alluded as early as 1906. Under the revolutionary dispensation, the "industrial development of China [would] be carried out along two lines: (1) by private enterprise and (2) by national undertaking. All matters that can be and are better carried out by private enterprise should be left to private hands which would be encouraged and fully protected by liberal laws. . . . All matters that cannot be taken up by private concerns and those that possess monopolistic character should be taken up as national undertakings. . . . The property thus created [would] be state-owned and [would] be managed for the benefit of the whole nation."[55]

These policies governing the process of industrialization constituted the substance of "the control of capital." Private enterprise was to operate freely within the expanding economy, but critical sectors of the economy and major undertakings were to be conducted by the planning and control agencies of

---

54. Sun, "Keng-che yao-yu ch'i-t'ien" [Land to the tillers], *KFCC* 2: 719-723; *SMCI*, pp. 187-200.
55. Sun, *International Development*, p. 135.

the state.[56] The state, furthermore, would assume tutelary obligation to insure a system of distribution that would minimally provide adequate—and gradually, approximately equal—welfare for all. Such a system would displace profit as the single object of enterprise and would "make nurture of the people its aim." Ultimately, the capitalist system of commodity production would be entirely displaced.[57] "In a nutshell," Sun was to insist, "it is my idea to make capitalism create socialism in China so that these two economic forces of human evolution will work side by side in future civilization."[58]

These complex programs of economic development and modernization would require, as we have seen, substantial capital and technological transfers from the more advanced nations. Such transactions would have to be undertaken under circumstances of equity and mutual respect. To insure such circumstances, China must have the military power to deter threat and the sovereign right to abrogate unequal treaties.[59] China, undertaking development, required the effective right to maintain a system of tariffs to protect nascent, and as yet noncompetitive, industries. Without the abrogation of unequal treaties, which denied China the sovereign right to determine its own trade and investment policies, economic relations with the more advanced powers would work to the nation's disadvantage.[60] Sun's continued insistence on the necessity of importing foreign capital, technology, and expertise[61] was always tempered by an equal insistence on China's political independence and military preparedness. Only "if China stood on an equal political basis with other nations could she compete freely with them in the economic field and hold her own. But as soon as foreign nations use political power as a shield for their economic designs, then China is at a loss how to resist or to compete successfully with them."[62]

---

56. Sun, "History of the Chinese Revolution," *Fundamentals*, p. 82.
57. Sun, *SMCI*, pp. 198-199.
58. Sun, *International Development*, p. 334.
59. Sun, *The Vital Problem*, pp. 6, 8-9, 29-32, 96, 115, 124, 136-137, 150-151, 171; cf. "The Kuomintang Declaration at Its First National Convention, January, 1924," and "Dr. Sun's Manifesto on the Northern Expedition, September 18, 1924," in Leonard S. Hsü, *Sun Yat-sen: His Political and Social Ideals* (Los Angeles: University of Southern California Press, 1932), pp. 120-141, 142-145.
60. Sun, *SMCI*, pp. 208-209; cf. "Statement on Establishment of the Central Bank of China. August 16, 1924," *Fundamentals*, p. 175. See also Yeh Shang-chih, *Minsheng ching-chi-hsueh* [Economics of people's livelihood], (Taipei: Lion Publishers, 1966).
61. Sun, "How to Develop Chinese Industry," *Fundamentals*, p. 187.
62. Sun, *SMCI*, p. 208.

For Sun, China's future could be assured only by the determined actions of the Chinese themselves. Armed with well-defined objectives and a programmatic guide to modernization and development, the Chinese could achieve economic and industrial maturity in "two or three decades." For Sun, the Chinese would have to provide the determination themselves. For his part, he imagined himself having delivered an ideology and a programmatic guide to development more realistic and more coherent than any other offered his contemporaries. More than a generation after his death, the defeated remnants of the revolutionary party he founded undertook to implement his policies in what was to be "a model province" of the China that Sun had unsuccessfully sought to unify and modernize. In 1949 the Kuomintang, committed to the program left by Sun Yat-sen, undertook the economic modernization and industrial development of Taiwan.

- background info for Taiwan's economic development
- "why Taiwan is a black swan"
- counterargument for dependency theory

II

Agriculture in the Economic Development of Taiwan

After more than two decades of conflict with local warlords, foreign invaders, and communist revolutionaries, the defeated Nationalist government of the Republic of China left the mainland of Asia and established itself in Taipei, Taiwan. By 1949 the Kuomintang heirs of Sun Yat-sen had few options other than to attempt to make Taiwan a "bastion" for the recovery of the nation they had lost. *"Japan's rice-bowl"*

But in 1949 the island of Taiwan had few of the properties of a bastion. It was an island in all but total economic disarray. For fifty years it had been a colony of Japan. It had served primarily as a food resource for the metropole, and trade and financial relations bound it almost exclusively to the Japanese homeland. With the advent of the Second World War, many Taiwanese were conscripted as soldiers or laborers into the Japanese armed forces, significantly reducing the manpower available for the labor-intensive agriculture that constituted the principal economic activity on the island. The decline in effective labor was coupled with a grievous loss in intermediate capital goods—primarily chemical fertilizers—essential to food crop production. Early in the Pacific conflict the Japanese could no longer secure the shipping lanes from the homeland to Taiwan, and the availability of fertilizers on Taiwan declined to 5 percent of the prewar level. Capital assets decayed for lack of maintenance, and with the loss of manpower the elaborate irrigation system, put together so painfully over half a century, began to disintegrate. The final blows fell with the extensive bombings of February-May 1945, as the Allies prepared for an amphibious invasion of the island. In a short time 65 percent of the industrial and infrastructural base of the island's economy was destroyed.

The defeat of Japan in 1945 saw the retrocesssion of the island to the Republic of China. On October 25, 1945, Taiwan was restored to Chinese administration. Taiwan's trade and financial ties with Japan were abruptly severed, further disrupting the economy by dislocating established market and credit patterns. The disorder was complicated by the repatriation to

Japan of twenty thousand technicians and managerial personnel, ten thousand professional workers, and forty thousand government officials. Their departure left vacant critical posts in the scientific, technical, and administrative structure of the island's economy.[1] The Japanese occupation had prevented the emergence of competent and dynamic administrators, scientists, and entrepreneurs among the Taiwanese, and the loss of just such personnel further degraded the war-ravaged economy.[2] All these factors accelerated the decline in crop yields already begun during the war. By 1946 agricultural productivity had declined to less than half that of 1937.[3]

The first contingents of Nationalist troops that landed on the war-ravaged and economically depressed island in 1945 and 1946 were dispirited and defeated remnants of the armies that had fought the Japanese and insurgents for almost a decade. They brought disease, disorder, and corruption. Nationalist forces confiscated a large share of the island's assets for their own use or for transport to the mainland, where the final resistance to the communist revolution was being attempted. Under the pressure of these and other exactions commodity prices on the island rose, between November 1945 and January 1947, about 700 percent for food, 1,400 percent for fuel and construction materials, and 25,000 percent for agricultural fertilizer. By the beginning of 1946 the American advisors on Taiwan were predicting serious indigenous uprisings against the Nationalist forces.[4] In February 1947 riots broke out in the urban centers of Taiwan, and for weeks the native population controlled the major cities on the island. Only in mid-March did troop reinforcements of the 21st Division, Shanghai, manage to put down the rebellion and secure the island once again.

The brutality with which the insurrection was repressed was to leave indelible scars. Nonetheless, one benefit did result. General Chen Yi, responsible for the behavior of the Nationalist forces during Taiwan's treatment as a "militarily administered territory," was replaced by Wei Tao-ming, who changed the island's status to that of a province of China—as it had been before the Japanese occupation in 1895.

1. Chien-sheng Shih, "Economic Development in Taiwan After the Second World War," *Weltwirtschaftliches Archiv* 100, no. 1 (1968): 116.
2. Samuel P. S. Ho, *Economic Development of Taiwan* (New Haven: Yale University Press, 1978), pp. 101-102.
3. Erik Thorbecke, "Agricultural Development," in *Economic Growth and Structural Change in Taiwan,* ed. Walter Galenson (Ithaca, N.Y.: Cornell University Press, 1979), p. 135, Table 2.2; Ching-yuan Lin, *Industrialization in Taiwan, 1946-72* (New York: Praeger, 1973), p. 29.
4. Douglas Mendel, *The Politics of Formosan Nationalism* (Berkeley and Los Angeles: University of California Press, 1970), chap. 2.

By the end of 1949, after the forces of Mao Tse-tung began their final southern campaign, the Nationalist government transferred its seat to Taipei, animated by a decision to make the island a "redoubt," a fortress that might withstand the military power of the communist forces on the mainland. In January 1949, in anticipation of that decision, Chiang Kai-shek had replaced Wei with General Chen Cheng, in an effort to restore the integrity of Nationalist rule on the island.

The choice of Chen Cheng heralded something more than a simple changing of the guard. The Nationalist leadership recognized that the circumstances required something more than suppressing political dissidence on Taiwan. By the beginning of 1949 it was becoming obvious that Taiwan might have to serve as a support base for the Kuomintang for some considerable time. Resistance on the mainland was becoming increasingly difficult. Should resistance collapse, Taiwan might serve as a staging area for recovery of the mainland. But if that were to be the case, the island would have to be not only secure, but economically viable as well. The political leadership on the island would be required not only to stabilize the population, but also to enhance the island's ability to survive in isolation.

The selection of Chen Cheng to undertake the reconstruction of Taiwan's economy indicated that the Nationalists contemplated more than the simple restoration of political and military control over the island. It was evident that the authorities appreciated the necessity of providing at least minimal welfare satisfactions to the rural population. On the mainland the forces of Mao Tse-tung had exploited the accumulation of rural grievances.[5] Such grievances had fatally undermined the position of the Kuomintang on the mainland. It was equally clear, however, that something more than a program of rural population control and simple economic rehabilitation was intended for Taiwan. If that was all that the authorities sought, the Japanese had left them all the elements of a successful population management policy and a pattern of economic controls that afforded considerable return on investments. For half a hundred years the Japanese had controlled Taiwan by forging a connection with the landholders on the island and supplementing that connection with extensive police controls. With such a system the Japanese had successfully dominated Taiwan, increased its agricultural yield significantly, and extracted considerable profit from the relationship. If control and agricultural productivity were its sole concerns, there was no prima facie reason why the Kuomintang could not have simply revamped and revitalized the Japanese system to its own purposes.

---

5. Chen Cheng, *Land Reform in Taiwan* (Taipei: China Publishing, 1961), pp. 47, 90.

In fact, by the beginning of 1949 the political and military goals of the Kuomintang required something more than effective control and agricultural rehabilitation on Taiwan. The Kuomintang had to contemplate the possibility of creating at least the rudiments of an industrial base on the island to support a demanding military establishment.[6] The Japanese control system, with its basically agricultural economy, could hardly serve such ends. Circumstances forced the political leadership on Taiwan to begin a program of overall economic development.

Chiang Kai-shek chose Chen to assume critical responsibilities in putting together such a program. Chen had been one of Sun Yat-sen's "loyalists" at the Whampoa Military Academy and a close confidant of Chiang. He had undertaken the leadership of the Society for the Study of Sun Yat-senism while at the academy and was ideologically committed to the inherited doctrines of min-sheng. With the first intellectuals who had collected around Sun, he had learned from Henry George that resolving the "land question" was prerequisite to any indigenous "economic progress." Taking "rent in taxation for public purposes," George had argued, would "further advances in productive power, and the tendency in this direction would be greatly accelerated."[7] Like all of Sun's followers Chen understood that any effort to modernize and industrialize an economy would require a land policy that would release capital from traditional pursuits for employment in the modern sector.

Sun had identified primary production—agriculture and mining—as the basis of all other economic activity.[8] As we have seen, Sun's original land policy was calculated not only to provide relief for the rural population of China but also to release capital, long immobilized in landholdings, for industrial and commercial use. He anticipated not only increasing yields from agriculture through major land reform, but institutional techniques that would transfer the profits from that increasing yield into the country's emerging industries. All of that had become so evident to the ideologues of the Kuomintang that in 1943, when Chiang Kai-shek wrote a brief account of "Chinese Economic Theory,"[9] he simply reiterated Sun's plan of

6. Chiang Kai-shek had long contemplated making Taiwan a "redoubt" in the event of a military defeat. After the collapse of the defenses in the North, the Kuomintang prepared to remove the principal assets of the Republic of China to Taipei. The transfer of bank funds was completed by February 1949. See Brian Crozier, *The Man Who Lost China* (New York: Charles Scribner's Sons, 1976), chap. 21; and Hollington K. Tong, *Chiang Kai-shek* (Taipei: China Publishing, 1953), pp. 452f.
7. Henry George, *Progress and Poverty* (New York: Schalkenbach, 1953), pp. 272, 413, 433, 442; cf. p. 456.
8. Sun Yat-sen, "How to Develop Chinese Industry," in *Fundamentals of National Reconstruction* (Taipei: Sino-American Publishing Co., 1953), p. 190.
9. It is clear that Professor Tao Hsi-sheng played a considerable role in drafting the

economic development predicated on the necessary resolution of the land problem.[10] A coherent land policy was, in his judgment, the necessary condition for both rural stability and industrial and commercial development.[11]

Such a policy would involve systematic cadastral surveys, effective land redistribution, a program of water conservancy, and an extension of irrigation facilities. As Sun had before him, Chiang spoke of the necessity of technological innovation and the introduction of agrobiological extension services to the farmer to insure the use of the most modern, scientific methods of farm production. Like Sun, he advocated developing a wide transport and communications infrastructure to serve rural needs—all in the effort to improve per capita and total agricultural productivity.[12] All of that, in turn, would have to be undertaken in conformity with a program that would provide for the intersectoral transfer of capital from the agrarian to the modernizing and industrial sector. Under such a program "commercial capital [would] be invested in industry instead." For Chiang, like Sun, the land policy was understood "in terms of agricultural-industrial, and more especially of agricultural-commercial, relations in order to achieve a real solution. The solution of the land problem [would] not only put an end to commercial profiteering and the enlargement of land holding, but [would] also facilitate the industrialization of China."[13]

Ideally, agricultural policy would not only create circumstances in which there would be net capital transfers from the traditional to the modern sectors of the economy, but it would enhance the raw materials production necessary for industrial growth and provide the increases in per capita consumption in the rural areas that would expand the market for industrial products as well.[14] Native industries, protected from foreign competition by import tariffs, could establish themselves and lay the foundations for China's economic and industrial growth.[15]

This was the intellectual baggage with which Chen Cheng arrived in Taiwan. He was convinced that the failure "to carry out Dr. Sun Yat-sen's land to the tiller ideal while . . . still on the mainland" was one of the principal reasons for the defeat of the Kuomintang. More than that, in his

text, but it is equally clear that the central ideas contained in the exposition were Chiang's. Cf. Crozier, *The Man Who Lost China,* pp. 246-247.

10. Chiang Kai-shek, "Chinese Economic Theory," in *China's Destiny* (New York: Roy, 1947), pp. 242-245.

11. Ibid., p. 258.

12. Ibid., pp. 272-274.

13. Ibid., p. 285.

14. Ibid., p. 287; in this context compare John W. Mellor, *The Economics of Agricultural Development* (Ithaca, N.Y.: Cornell University Press, 1966).

15. Chiang, "Chinese Economic Theory," p. 279.

judgment the "implementation of land reform [was] not only basic to the betterment of the people's livelihood and the promotion of political social stability," but it provided the "motive force for the furtherance of economic development and industrialization."[16] Chen assumed his responsibilities on Taiwan with a clear appreciation of Sun's policies concerning economic growth and modernization.

Ideological resolve, however, could not supply the foreign capital assistance and technological transfers called for in Sun's original program. Sun and the intellectuals around him had made the availability of international capital a critical part of their program. They argued that once the constraints and impostures produced by unequal treaties were eliminated, a developing China could enter into bilateral and multilateral trade and assistance programs that would foster its modernization and industrialization.

In 1949 the defeated Republic of China seemed to offer few investment opportunities to foreign capital and few political or strategic benefits to the United States that might prompt economic or technological assistance. The United States gave every evidence of desiring discreet withdrawal from its long relationship with the Republic of China.

Without foreign assistance, the Republic of China on Taiwan probably would not survive, much less undertake successful economic modernization and growth. Not only was there the constant threat of military attack by Mao's forces, but the economy of Taiwan suffered major strains produced by the deficit financing needed to maintain one of the largest standing armies in Asia. If the Kuomintang was to survive, it would have to be supported by one of the major industrial powers.

Chiang Kai-shek, fully cognizant of Sun's convictions concerning China's necessity to ally with one of the major powers during its transition from an underdeveloped to a developed nation, anticipated that the remnants of the Republic of China, irrespective of the immediate circumstances of 1949, could expect to ally itself with the anticommunist forces of the Western world against the growing threat of communist military and political expansion. Even while the economic and financial circumstances of the Republic of China appeared all but hopeless,[17] Chiang anticipated the possibility of reestablishing an alliance with the United States in what he anticipated would be the Western world's resistance against communism.

During this critical period the Soviet Union increasingly revealed itself to the United States as a real antagonist—and the communist regime on the Chinese mainland, for whatever reason, aligned itself with Moscow. In

16. Chen, *Land Reform in Taiwan*, pp. xii, xiii.
17. International Monetary Fund, *International Financial Statistics* (Washington, D.C.: International Monetary Fund, April 1969).

January 1950 Mao Tse-tung's forces seized the American consular offices in Peking. In June the Korean War commenced, and in July 200,000 communist Chinese troops were deployed along the North Korean border. These events increased American interest in Taiwan as a strategic logistic base in the event of the expansion of hostilities in the Pacific. With the subsequent involvement of Chinese communist "volunteers" in the Korean fighting, American interest in, and commitment to, the defense and security of Taiwan increased. American military and economic aid began to flow into the Republic of China on Taiwan, first to bring economic, political, and social stability, and then to help fuel economic growth and development. Chiang had gambled on such an eventuality when he charged Chen Cheng with the responsibility of initiating a program of economic development on Taiwan.

Thus, by the end of 1950 and the beginning of 1951 all the elements of a developmental program for Taiwan had been put into place. Animated by the program left by Sun Yat-sen, the Kuomintang undertook the economic modernization and industrial development of Taiwan. The program involved initial stages requiring a resolution of the problems that beset the countryside through redistributing assets and redividing land and concurrently redirecting capital from the agricultural sector, while increasing yield and maintaining, or enhancing, demand in the traditional sector. The subsequent stage would involve creating and expanding local industries via a stringent policy of import substitution and sheltered growth. American assistance would service both stages with capital concessions and loans, technology transfers, technical assistance, and administrative counseling.

When the American aid program for Taiwan began in the early 1950s, it was received with a "competence, energy, development-mindedness, and cooperative spirit" that distinguished its reception from that accorded by almost every other aid recipient.[18] That it was so received was as much a consequence of long familiarity with the program of development we now identify with Sun Yat-sen as it was a function of native competence and energy. More than "some aspects of Sun Yat-sen's Three People's Principles can be read into Nationalist rule" on Taiwan;[19] the entire program was not only infused with the developmental spirit characteristic of his ideology, it embodied most of its critical components.

In the early months of 1949, in anticipation of eventual American aid, the political authorities on Taiwan began a program of economic development. The circumstances surrounding their rule on Taiwan, coupled with

---

18. Neil Jacoby, *U.S. Aid to Taiwan* (New York: Praeger, 1966), pp. 225-226.
19. John Israel, "Politics on Formosa," in *Formosa Today,* ed. Mark Mancall (New York: Praeger, 1964), p. 59.

the necessity to impart a sense of reality to their political and strategic goals, moved the Kuomintang to undertake the first phase of Sun's program for economic growth and industrialization. That phase required a general rent reduction for tenant farmers in the rural areas. That part of Sun's program had been one of the planks of the Kuomintang as early as 1930. In that year the central government of the newly united Republic of China had promulgated a land law which provided (among other things) that farm rentals should not exceed 37.5 percent of the total annual yield of agricultural main crops. In conformity with that legislation, rent reductions were attempted in Kwangtung, Hunan, Hupeh, and Chekiang provinces. In Hupeh, Chen Cheng was reasonably successful in implementing the rent reduction legislation.[20]

Although the efforts on the mainland of China had failed, in 1949 the Kuomintang had every incentive to try once again. With the full approval of the Central Committee of the Kuomintang, and the express instructions of Chiang Kai-shek, Chen Cheng, immediately upon his arrival, was instructed to decree a reduction of agrarian land rents in Taiwan to a sum no greater than 37.5 percent of the total annual yield of the main farm crop.

The measurable effect of the decree (and its subsequent embodiment into law) was immediate. Enforcement was begun in April 1949 and concluded in September of the same year. A survey of 1,439 tenant families in 43 districts and townships of the seven counties of Taipei, Hsinchu, Taichung, Tainan, Kaohsiung, Taitung, and Hualien found that land rents averaged 56.8 percent of the harvest of 1948. Some farm rentals in Hsinchu were found to be as high as 70 percent of the annual yield. With the edict on rent reduction, all those were to be reduced to no more than 37.5 percent of total yearly production. By May 1949, 302,000 farm families had entered into new lease contracts governed by the new rent reduction legislation. Of the total cultivated land area of 2,018,760 acres on Taiwan, 613,000 acres were affected by the rent reductions. By 1952, when the program was completed, it involved 43 percent of the total number of farm households and more than 29 percent of the total cultivated land.

Almost immediately thereafter, the Nationalist government began a program to transfer ownership of land to actual tillers by selling some of the public land possessed by the central and provincial governments, which amounted to about 20 percent of the cultivated land surface of Taiwan. The price set on public land was 2.5 times the annual yield of the principal crops

---

20. Cf. Chen, *Land Reform in Taiwan,* pp. 18-19. For Chen's views on land reform see Chen Cheng, *An Approach to China's Land Reform* (Taipei: Chen Cheng Publisher, 1951). See also W. G. Goddard, *Formosa: A Study in Chinese History* (Edinburgh: R. & R. Clark, n.d.), pp. 185-194.

and was to be paid in twenty installments over ten years. At the conclusion of the program more than 171,700 acres were sold to 139,688 farm families.

In January 1951 a systematic ownership survey was undertaken by a joint Sino-American commission (the Joint Commission on Rural Reconstruction) in anticipation of the enactment of further land reform legislation designed to transfer the ownership of surplus land from landlords to tillers. In July 1952 the draft of 33 articles, which was to serve as the prototype of the subsequent legislation that would redistribute land ownership on Taiwan, was submitted to the Provincial Assembly. On January 20, 1953, the omnibus legislation designed to provide land to actual tillers became law. The government then undertook compulsory purchase of all land that exceeded the prescribed retention limit (three *chia*, or 7.16 acres) to be sold to the tenants who were the actual tillers. By December 1953 the compulsory purchase and resale of land, involving 16.4 percent of the total cultivated land surface of Taiwan, was complete. More than 344,000 acres of land were purchased and resold to 194,800 farm families. This redistribution, coupled with the sale of public lands, involved 24.5 percent of the total cultivated acreage of Taiwan.[21]

Landlords were compensated at a value set at 2.5 times the annual yield of their excess land, 70 percent of the compensation coming in commodity (rice and sweet potato) bonds and the remainder in shares of stock in four government enterprises (the Taiwan Cement Corporation, Taiwan Pulp and Paper Corporation, Taiwan Industrial and Mining Corporation, and Taiwan Agricultural and Forestry Development Corporation). The commodity bonds paid a 4 percent annual interest, and both bond principal and interest were to be amortized in twenty equal semiannual installments. Tenants purchased the land from the government at the price paid by the government to the former owners. The purchase price was paid at a 4 percent annual interest and in direct payments in kind for rice paddies or in cash payments for land devoted to sweet potato cultivation.

By the end of the rent reduction, public land sales, and land-to-the-tillers programs, more than 43 percent of all farm families on Taiwan had benefited by the statutory reduction in share-cropping fees (about 20 percent purchased public lands) and almost 48 percent of all farm households had profited from land redistribution. Almost half of Taiwan's farm families, or about 75 percent of tenant and part-tenant households, were able to purchase at least some land. As a consequence, the number of tenant and part-tenant farm households as a share of total farm households on Taiwan declined from 41 percent in 1947 to 21 percent in 1953, to decline still further to 10

---

21. See Cheng, *China's Land Reform*, chap. 4; Ho, *Economic Development of Taiwan*, pp. 162-165.

percent in 1970. In accordance with Sun's policies of land reform, more and more tenant farmers became owner-cultivators, and a ceiling was imposed on land rents. Beyond that, the effects anticipated by Sun, less easy to isolate and quantify, radiated throughout the island economy.[22]

Most analysts seem prepared to argue that land redistribution and rent reduction sparked the rapid increase in agricultural production that characterized the fifteen years that followed the program.[23] Because farmers could work their own property, and because increases in yield no longer were paid out in increased rents, tillers were not only more disposed to employ more capital and the most advanced agricultural technology (new crop varieties, new pesticides, and increased use of fertilizer), but to work harder (restoring the irrigation systems, double cropping cultivated land, and using better crop rotation systems) to increase total farm productivity. This disposition would help to explain why from 1950 to 1955 the index for fixed capital investment per agricultural worker almost doubled and the use of chemical and organic fertilizers increased at annual percentage rates of about 5.7 and 3.3 respectively. In 1950 the demand for chemical fertilizers was about 290,000 metric tons; it rose to about 580,000 metric tons in 1955, 610,000 metric tons in 1960, and 766,000 metric tons in 1965.[24] There was a comparable increase in the use of insecticides and fungicides during the same period.

At the same time the number of man-days per agricultural worker applied to the land rose from 159 in 1950 to 184 in 1960 to 194 in 1970. While the actual number of agricultural workers rose by roughly 1 percent per annum during this period, the number of total man-days of agricultural labor rose about 4 percent annually.[25] The consequence was a full restoration and perfection of the irrigation system and increased multiple cropping, so that crop area increased 2.25 percent annually while total cultivated land

22. See Doreen Warriner, *Land Reform and Economic Development* (Cairo: National Bank of Egypt, 1955).

23. H. S. Tang and S. C. Hsieh, "Land Reform and Agricultural Development in Taiwan," *The Malayan Economic Review* 6, no. 1 (April 1961): 18-57; but see Ronald J. Herring, "Share Tenancy and Economic Efficiency: The South Asian Case," *Peasant Studies* 7, no. 4 (Fall 1978): 225-249.

24. These figures are adapted from T. H. Lee and Y. E. Chen, *Growth Rates of Taiwan Agriculture, 1911-1972* (Taipei: Joint Commission on Rural Reconstruction [JCRR], 1975); T. H. Shen, ed., *Agriculture's Place in the Strategy of Development: The Taiwan Experience* (Taipei: JCRR, 1974); and Kowie Chang, ed., *Economic Development in Taiwan* (Taipei: Cheng Chung Publisher, 1968), p. 189, Table 3-36. For a general survey see Joint Commission on Rural Reconstruction, *JCRR and Agricultural Development in Taiwan 1948-1978* (Taipei: JCRR, 1978).

25. Adapted from Thorbecke, "Agricultural Development," p. 150; cf. p. 151, Table 2.8.

increased only 0.4 percent. Agricultural production per worker (computed in Taiwan dollars at 1935-1937 value) rose from $278 in 1950 to $327 in 1955 and to $385 in 1960. The per hectare (ha. = 2.471 acres) yields of rice improved from 1,845 kg./ha. in 1950 to 2,151 in 1955 and 3,038 in 1965. Sweet potato production improved from 9,443 kg./ha. in 1950 to 13,377 kg./ha. in 1965. Corn, wheat, soybean, and sugarcane yields all similarly improved.[26] Production of rice in Taiwan increased by about 70 percent in the two decades following the land reform. (Between 1945 and 1976 annual rice yield increased from 639,000 to 2,713,000 metric tons.) In 1965 the aggregate agricultural output of crops (including livestock, fisheries, and forest products) was 2.6 times that of the 1950-1952 average. The annual growth rate for aggregate yield averaged 5.2 percent for the period 1953 through 1968.[27] The increase in agricultural productivity not only made it possible for Taiwan to meet the domestic food requirements of a population increasing at more than 3 percent annually (from 8 million in 1952 to 13.5 million in 1968), it provided a substantial surplus for export.

Whatever the effect of land distribution on individual and collective incentives—and however much or however little those incentives contributed to agricultural development—land reform significantly altered patterns of income distribution. The relationship between income and land tenure is generally recognized, and the fact that land reform made land ownership both possible and secure for the majority of rural households assured them more equitable access to future income streams. Land was sold to farmers at low prices and on easy terms (particularly in view of the credit market conditions in the early 1950s). If one assumes that Taiwanese agricultural yield would have increased at the same rate without as with land reform, it is estimated that farm incomes on the island would have risen by about 16 percent in the period between 1948 and 1959. If it is assumed that under the same conditions landlords could be made to share in productive costs, then farm incomes would have risen by about 40 percent during the same period. With rent reduction, however, farm incomes increased by more than 90 percent. The income of the farm tenant who became an owner-cultivator under the land-to-the-tiller program increased by 107 percent. Furthermore, with the completion of land payments (in 1963) farm incomes automatically increased by the amount equal to the annual amortization and interest. Assuming that agricultural development would have proceeded at the same pace without land reform as it did with reform, about 85 percent of farm

26. Shen, *Agriculture's Place,* p. 423, Table 9. For the data on agricultural production per worker, see T. H. Lee, *Intersectoral Capital Flows in the Economic Development of Taiwan, 1895-1960* (Ithaca, N.Y.: Cornell University Press, 1971), p. 13, Table 1.
27. T. H. Shen, "The Mechanism for Agricultural Planning," in *Agriculture's Place,* p. 33; see Lee and Chen, *Growth Rates of Taiwan Agriculture 1911-1972.*

income that accrued to farmers because of reform would have gone to landlords instead.[28]

The landlord class suffered the most from the land reform programs. Quite independent of their loss of future incomes, landlords were compelled to sell their land at a price equivalent to 2.5 times the annual yield of the major crop, when estimates of the average market value of fields at that time was four to six times the annual yield. The land transfers thus cost the landlords a sum estimated to have been approximately 13 percent of Taiwan's gross domestic product in 1952 (2.2 billion in New Taiwan dollars). Moreover, the government commodity bonds provided as compensation for confiscated lands earned only 4 percent interest, when the real market interest rate ranged from 30 to 50 percent and in preferential interest rate savings deposits reached 125 percent. Finally, many landlords sold those bonds at prices substantially lower than their nominal value, further compounding their losses.

As Sun Yat-sen and those around him had anticipated, one of the most important economic consequences of these changes was a capital outflow from the agricultural to the nonagricultural sector amounting to about 22 percent of the total value of agricultural production between 1950 and 1955.[29] This was accomplished not only by forced land sales but, in part, by the increase in real farm incomes that commenced with land reform. In the prewar period (1936-1940) the average farmer spent 92 percent of his income. In the period between 1956 and 1960 spending had fallen to 80 percent. In effect, between 1940 and 1956 the average moneysaving-consumption ratio in rural households rose from 8 to 10 percent. The substantial savings that accumulated among farm families in the 1950s could be largely attributed to the income redistribution effected by the rent reduction and land reform programs of 1949 and 1953.[30] Financial institutions transferred that capital to the capital-scarce industrial sector.

Coupled with compulsory land sales and high voluntary savings, a number of government policies ensured a high net capital outflow from the agricultural to the nonagricultural sector. One such policy involved government control over the marketing of rice. Regulations made land taxes and land payments payable in rice, instituted a schedule of compulsory rice sales to the government, and established a rice/fertilizer barter system through

---

28. Ho, *Economic Development of Taiwan,* pp. 168-170; Martin M. C. Yang, *Socio-Economic Results of Land Reform in Taiwan* (Honolulu: East-West Center Press, 1970), chaps. 7 and 9; Thorbecke, "Agricultural Development," p. 176.
29. T. H. Lee, *Strategies for Transferring Agricultural Surplus Under Different Agricultural Situations in Taiwan,* mimeographed (Taipei: JCRR, 1971).
30. T. H. Lee, *Intersectoral Capital Flows,* p. 120.

which farmers obtained critically needed fertilizers only by providing rice in exchange. All these rice collections were obtained at government prices that were considerably lower than prevailing market prices. As a consequence, the government received "invisible" revenues equivalent to the difference between the government price and the market price, multiplied by the total amount of rice obtained.[31] Those revenues became one of the principal sources of government funds.

The rice/fertilizer barter system was the most important single program in the government's rice collection enterprise. To reduce the loss of foreign exchange through the import of chemical fertilizers, the government controlled fertilizer imports and undertook the creation of a domestic fertilizer industry. Farmers were obliged to purchase fertilizer from the government at government rates with payment in rice. Since the price of government fertilizer was higher than the international market price—and since the government purchase price of rice was lower than the prevailing domestic market price—the barter system was a major mechanism for transferring capital from agriculture to the remainder of the national economy. Farmers thus were compelled to underwrite not only the development of a domestic fertilizer industry,[32] but other developmental projects as well.

In 1955 the government on Taiwan collected about 74 percent of all rice marketed. Since that time government intervention in the rice market has remained substantial. In 1969 about 44 percent of the total was obtained by the government through land taxes, rents, rice/fertilizer barter exchanges, and compulsory sales at prices 20 to 30 percent below open market prices. As a consequence, the government was able to fix terms of trade throughout the growth period that insured relatively low cost comestibles to its population, stabilized rice prices, and secured a high net outflow of capital from the agricultural to the modernizing sectors of the economy.[33] Government agrarian policies after land reform provided the mechanisms for the net transfer of resources from agriculture to the modern sectors of the economy by divesting landlords of their holdings at government prices, by marketing

31. Shirley W. Y. Kuo, "Effects of Land Reform, Agricultural Pricing Policy and Economic Growth on Multiple Crop Diversification in Taiwan," *Philippines Economic Journal* 14, nos. 1-2 (1975): 159-164; see Kuo-shu Liang and T. H. Lee, "Taiwan," in *The Economic Development of East and Southeast Asia,* ed. Shinichi Ichimura (Honolulu: East-West Center Press, 1975), p. 305.
32. Thorbecke, "Agricultural Development," p. 181; T. H. Lee and T. H. Shen, "Agriculture as a Base for Socio-Economic Development," in *Agriculture's Place,* pp. 291-300; A. Y. C. Koo, *The Role of Land Reform in Economic Development* (New York: Praeger, 1968).
33. Sung-hsing Wang and Raymond Apthorpe, *Rice Farming in Taiwan: Three Village Studies* (Taipei: Academia Sinica, 1974), pp. 2-3.

rice at government prices, and by bartering fertilizer, the essential modern agricultural input, at government rates.

These policies also provided for increased income equity throughout the economy, afforded risk reduction to farmers by stabilizing market prices, and helped reduce inflationary pressures in an expanding productive system. The land reform not only caused capital transfers from the agricultural to the modern sector, the attendant redistribution of assets and income stimulated the island's industrialization efforts through the increased demand of farm households created by rising rural incomes. Thus directly and indirectly, agriculture was made a major domestic resource for capital formation.

To make the growth dividends from agriculture fuel industrialization and economic development without generating social and political dissidence in the countryside, substantial benefits were provided to farm households to supplement the increasing income that attended the process. A number of such benefits were supplied almost immediately. In the first place, the entire program was supervised closely by the Sino-American Joint Commission on Rural Reconstruction to ensure that modern agrobiological and technological assistance was made equally available to all farmers. Moreover, the irrigation associations, sponsored by the government, assured all farmers of adequate water supplies, something critical to farming on Taiwan. Furthermore, by 1965 the government, through its own agencies or government-sponsored farmers' associations, supplied 65 percent of all agricultural loans under strictly controlled conditions. Before the land reform private moneylenders had provided 82 percent of the credit available to farmers at rates that were all too often disabling, if not ruinous.[34] In 1950 farmers could secure short-term commercial loans at 3.45 percent per month. With government control and the availability of credit through the cooperative farmers' associations, the rate fell to 1.2 percent per month by March 1964.

The rice/fertilizer barter system, under the provisions of Provincial Food Bureau allocation, ensured all farmers equal access to the limited supply of fertilizers. In most developing market economies where critical agricultural inputs—credit, water, and fertilizer—are in short supply, almost invariably the wealthier cultivators, with the larger holdings, obtain them. With that advantage the wealthier strata of the rural population increase their control over local credit, alienate smallholders from their land, and are in a position further to exploit impoverished agricultural laborers.[35] Land reform and close government supervision made all that impossible on Taiwan. The

34. R. P. Christensen, *Taiwan's Agricultural Development* (Washington, D.C.: Government Printing Office, 1968), p. 57.
35. Keith Griffin, *The Political Economy of Agrarian Change* (Cambridge, Mass.: Harvard University Press, 1974), p. 30.

political authorities were following Sun Yat-sen's injunction that "class conflicts between small and large farmers . . . be avoided."[36]

Coupled with these benefits, American aid assisted the rural population, directly and indirectly. During the period of major agricultural expansion (1950-1965), the rural areas were special beneficiaries of American foreign aid; $1.5 billion (about $100 million per year) was obligated to the Republic of China on Taiwan. About 37 percent of that aid, and 44 percent of U.S. dollar aid, went to infrastructural development—directly benefiting the rural population.

During that period huge commitments were made to electric power, transportation, and communications development.[37] In fact, American aid constituted 74 percent of all investments made in infrastructural development between 1950 and 1965. Almost 70 percent of the U.S. capital assistance grants and loans went to Taipower, the government's electrical power industry, which greatly expanded its hydroelectric and thermoelectric generating and distributing facilities. While most power output was designated for industrial use, enough was made available so that virtually all farm households had electricity by the end of the growth period. By 1970 almost every farm household had sewing machines and electric fans; nearly 80 percent had electric pumps for domestic water use (and had had since about 1967); nearly 50 percent had television sets; and 10 percent had refrigerators.[38]

Moreover, by the 1970s infrastructural investment had been used to stabilize and develop irrigation and drainage systems. More than 1,000 kilometers of canals in the Chianan irrigation area, for example, had been lined by that time, rotational irrigation had been extended to more than 120,000 ha. of paddy fields throughout the island, 726 deep wells had been drilled in central and southern Taiwan, more than 5,000 ha. of waste land and 4,000 ha. of tidal land had been reclaimed, and water reservoirs had been constructed at Shihmen, Tapu, Paiho, Houlung, and Tsengwen.[39]

U.S. aid and technical assistance also was instrumental in developing Taiwan's public school system and health services in the rural areas. After 1950 fifteen years of rural education succeeded in transforming Taiwan's agricultural population into one of the most literate in Asia. By 1960 92 percent of all school-age children in the rural areas of Taiwan attended six years of free, compulsory education. The high rate of literacy allowed the

36. Cf. Walter P. Falcon, "Lessons and Issues in Taiwan's Development," in *Agriculture's Place,* p. 271.
37. Jacoby, *U.S. Aid to Taiwan,* pp. 49, 176.
38. Wang and Apthorpe, *Rice Farming in Taiwan,* p. 37.
39. Han Lih-wu, *Taiwan Today* (Taipei: Cheng Chung Publisher, 1977), p. 100.

extensive use of modern means of communication to diffuse new skills that would upgrade rural life.[40] The extension of health and sanitation facilities to the rural areas enabled those who worked the land to enjoy the improved health and increased longevity that characterize the development of Taiwan. In effect, "health, sanitation, and education; caloric intake; overall consumption and other indices of welfare in the countryside have increased through the years in tandem with surplus extraction."[41]

Thus, under the developmental program of the Kuomintang, agriculture underwrote modernization and industrialization through net capital transfers from the farm to the modern sectors of the economy. The agricultural sector supplied much of the domestic capital on Taiwan and made up a substantial part of the island's international trade deficits. Between 1953 and 1962 the most binding constraint on Taiwan's development was the dearth of foreign exchange. During that period agricultural production not only met the domestic food requirements of a rapidly growing population but provided a surplus for exports sufficient to finance at least half of the total imports of the island. Agriculture, in conjunction with U.S. economic aid, thus financed the early industrialization of the Republic of China on Taiwan.[42] For all that, per capita and household farm incomes increased, and welfare and life-enhancement benefits were made more readily available to the countryside.

That the first phase of Taiwan's development was so successful is at least in part attributable to its having been initiated by "a group of people . . . who had a relatively clear conception of the form agricultural development should take."[43] That relatively clear conception, in substantial part, was the product of a long familiarity with the developmental ideology of Sun Yat-sen.

More than half a century ago Sun argued that resolution of the land problem was essential to any program of economic development and industrialization. He saw a complex program of land taxation, rent reduction, and land to the tillers as providing the mechanisms that would make rural resources available for capital formation in China. When the Kuomintang established itself on Taiwan and implemented his program, it found that rent

40. See Ho, *Economic Development of Taiwan,* p. 178; for statistics on education in general, see Henry Y. Wan, "Manpower, Industrialization and Export-Led Growth—the Taiwan Experience," in *Growth, Distribution and Social Change: Essays on the Economy of the Republic of China,* ed. Yuan-li Wu and Kung-chia Yeh (Baltimore: University of Maryland School of Law, 1978), p. 166, Table 12; for rural education, see Yang, *Socio-Economic Results,* pp. 373-378.
41. Alice H. Amsden, "Taiwan's Economic History," *Modern China* 5, no. 3 (July 1979): 359.
42. Liang and Lee, "Taiwan," p. 322.
43. Thorbecke, "Agricultural Development," p. 204.

reduction caused a precipitous decline in the value of agricultural land.[44] If Sun's proposal to impose a tax on the unearned increments on land was meant to transfer capital from the rural to the modernizing sectors of the economy, the declining value of agricultural land that followed rent reduction offered little occasion for its accomplishment. The consequence on Taiwan was that the land tax, identified as the "equalization of land rights" in Sun's ideology, was imposed only on some urban properties where, as a consequence of urbanization, land values rose.[45]

Harold Schiffrin is correct in recognizing that Sun's policy of *p'ing-chün ti-ch'üan,* the "equalization of land rights," did not provide for land redistribution.[46] Its clear purpose was not to redistribute land but to allow governmental appropriation of all future increases in land values subsequent to the revolution. Those revenues would then be transferred to the modern sector as domestically-generated capital. But, in fact, land values would increase only as the economy expanded—a fact which meant that modernization and industrialization required some *initial* source of capital to spark the process. On Taiwan those assets were provided by the rent reduction and the land-to-the-tillers programs—programs quite independent of any government appropriation of unearned increments.

The land reform program implemented on Taiwan by the Kuomintang was thus a modified form of that put together by Sun. Nonetheless, the purposes of the program, to which the specific policies were instrumental, were those Sun identified as critical to the economic development and industrialization of China. Agriculture was to supply the essential resources for the capital accumulation without which economic development could not proceed. Moreover, the land policy would prevent those social and political ills that would otherwise attend material progress. The land program would reduce social disparities and substantially ameliorate income inequalities. It

---

44. From December 1948 to December 1949, as a consequence of rent reduction, the average value of paddy fields dropped by 19.4 percent and that of dry land by 42.3 percent. Chen, *Land Reform in Taiwan,* p. 45.

45. The urban land tax, identified as the statute on the "equalization of land rights," called for a progressive tax on land value and a 30 to 90 percent tax on future increments in urban land values. *Free China Weekly,* February 7, 1956. Chiang Kai-shek indicated, in October 1952, that the tax on "unearned increments" in land values would be applied only to urban sites where values were expected to escalate. "Fan-kung kang-or chi-pen lun" [The basic doctrine of anti-communism and resistance to the Soviets], *Chiang T'sung-T'ung yen-lun hui-pien* [Compilation of the speeches and articles of President Chiang], (Taipei: Central Publishing Company, 1956), 7: 66-67.

46. Harold Z. Schiffrin, "Sun Yat-sen's Early Land Policy," *Journal of Asian Studies* 16 (August 1957): 549.

would involve conjoint commitment to the expansion of irrigation and water conservancy systems, to a policy of afforestation, to the provision of agricultural extension services to the rural area, to the establishment of agricultural banks to afford easy credit to the tillers, and to the reclamation and rehabilitation of waste lands. These points, together with Sun's emphasis on infrastructural development and the cultivation of human resources through education and the extension of health services, make up the principal constituents of the agricultural developmental policies implemented on Taiwan.

The actual policies pursued by the Kuomintang on Taiwan comprised all of these points, combined with a clear recognition that so ambitious a program required the capital and technical assistance of the more advanced industrial states. Wei Yung was substantially correct when he maintained that "it was not until the Nationalists retreated to Taiwan that they were able to fully implement the various programs of land reform embedded in the Three Principles of the People (*San-min chu-i*)."[47] The success of that program fueled the next stage of development and industrialization—and once again it was Sun Yat-sen who provided the programmatic guide for its success.

47. Wei Yung, "Taiwan: A Modernizing Chinese Society," in *Taiwan in Modern Times,* ed. Paul K. T. Sih (New York: St. John's University Press, 1973), p. 459. See also Shih Chien-sheng, "The Min-sheng chu-i and the Economic Modernization in Taiwan," *China Forum* 4, no. 2 (July 1977): 79-100; Wan Yu-hsüan, *T'u-ti, nung-yeh chi ch'i t'a* [Land, agriculture and other considerations], (Taipei: Academia Sinica, 1977); Pien Yü-yüan and Shih Yi-hsing, *Ching-chi fa-chan te chieh-tuan yü keng-tse yu-ch'i-t'ien* [The stages of economic development and the land-to-the-tillers program], (Taipei: Academia Sinica, 1978).

III

Industrialization

Sun Yat-sen seemed clearly to recognize the dualistic structure of China's economy—a small, modern sector of nonagricultural pursuits coexisted alongside a basically agricultural economy. The development of the nation's economy would require gradually shifting the center from the agrarian to the modern sectors. Accomplishing that shift would require modernizing agriculture, generating transferable agricultural surplus, accumulating real capital to sustain nonagricultural employment, and finally, reallocating labor from agricultural to nonagricultural pursuits. Rather than embarking immediately on an effort to fabricate a heavy industrial base for such an economy to the neglect of agriculture, Sun proposed a systematic upgrading of agriculture, infrastructural development, mass education, an expansion of labor-intensive industries under a regime of tariff protection, and a final effort to create a heavy industrial foundation for a new society. An interventionist government would create an environment favorable to private economic activity by influencing foreign exchange, credit, trade, tariffs, and foreign investment incentives. These actions would condition the subsequent course of growth and income streams. In addition, the government would directly participate in the economy through public ownership of certain industries.

As we have seen, Sun foresaw that early in the process the authorities would have to install protective tariffs and import controls to insulate native industries—initially labor-intensive—against any "invasion of foreign goods." In the first stages of its development, China would have to impose restrictive tariffs on foreign imports and "put into effect a protective policy" that would permit "home industries . . . to develop."[1]

Chiang Kai-shek, as heir to Sun's policies, early committed the Kuomintang to a protectionist, import substitution policy during the first phase of industrial development.[2] In 1943 Chiang reiterated all the essentials of Sun's

1. Sun Yat-sen, *San-min chu-i* (Taipei: China Publishing, n. d.), p. 209. Cited as *SMCI.*
2. See Chiang Kai-shek, "Chinese Economic Theory," in *China's Destiny* (New

41

program of phased development and modernization.[3] Critical to that program, Chiang went on, was China's adoption of "a protectionist policy with regard to foreign trade, and a policy of economic planning with respect to her industrial development."[4] During the first phase of Chinese development, primary comestible and nondurable consumer production must be assured, rendered maximally efficient, and modernized through a policy of protection. Such a program of sheltered growth, administered by the state, was calculated to help "transform an agricultural into an industrial society."[5]

Along with a land reform and protectionist policy, Chiang, like Sun, committed himself to an aggressive and interventionist role for the tutelary state. Central to the convictions of Sun's *International Development of China* was the conception of the state as a central management agency for the entire economy.[6] State planning would be indicative rather than prescriptive because the program for development, by design, would involve a large private sector and an attendant market economy. Given such circumstances—as well as the necessity of seeking substantial foreign capital and entrepreneurial and technological expertise—government planning in China would proceed under the constraints implicit in allowing the operation of domestic and foreign private enterprise facilitated by "liberal laws."

York: Roy, 1947), pp. 259-262. The commitment to tariff control and import substitution had been explicit in Chiang's writings as early as 1928 and 1929. In a speech entitled "My Reflections on Customs Tariffs," Chiang maintained: "Our ability to escape from foreign economic bondage depends on our control over customs regulations. Our agricultural, industrial and commercial development is retarded. . . . The tariff regulations imposed upon us by foreign governments permits foreign products to overwhelm our own. Our imports exceed our exports and we incur losses in trade deficits. This is the most difficult constraint on our economic development. . . . We will continue to struggle for full control of our customs regulations. Our purpose is our national economic development. . . . The full control over our customs regulation was one of the objectives pursued by our Tsung-li [Sun Yat-sen] for years." *Chiang T'sung-t'ung yen-lun hui-pien* [Compilation of the speeches and articles of President Chiang], (Taipei: Central Publishing Company, 1956), 9: 127; cf. ibid., 9: 92.
3. Ibid., pp. 267-273, 283.
4. Ibid., p. 279.
5. Chiang Kai-shek, "Chapters on National Fecundity, Social Welfare, Education and Health and Happiness," *Supplement to San-min chu-i* (Taipei: China Publishing, n.d.), p. 218; cf. *SMCI*, pp. 208-209.
6. Sun Yat-sen, *International Development of China*, in *Kuo-fu ch'üan-chi* 5: 135. Cited as *KFCC;* cf. Sun, *SMCI*, pp. 158-160, 180-182; "How to Develop Chinese Industry," *Fundamentals of National Reconstruction* (Taipei: Sino-American Publishing, 1953), p. 189.

Planning, under such money and commodity market constraints, could only be indicative. The state would control financial institutions and enterprises of scale, but vast sectors of the system would respond to price signals provided by the market. Such a mixed economy would have to allow for the uncertainties that are the product of opportunity costs and factor advantages characteristic of open, or relatively open, markets. Sun early recognized that one of China's advantages was its abundance of cheap labor. China could attract foreign and domestic private venture capital with its low-cost labor.[7] A substantial part of Chinese development could thus be underwritten by foreign and private capital seeking advantage in producing goods at competitive prices for international trade.[8] Planning, as a consequence, would have to be suggestive rather than mandatory, flexible rather than rigid, providing and employing incentives and disincentives rather than issuing quotas and allocating resources, practices common to public planning in command economies.

Other than providing general economic plans, the tutelary state would be charged with protecting collective welfare throughout the process of economic development and industrialization. It would, in Sun's view, not only foster the establishment and growth of initially cost-inefficient industries and provide for balanced growth, but it would attempt to provide for more equitable income and welfare distribution. In this latter regard, Sun Yat-sen advocated decentralization of industrial development in China to ensure the modernization and economic maturation of *all* areas of the country, as well as more equitable distribution of the attendant benefits.[9] Conjoined with currency regulation, tax reform, and land redistribution, the state would ensure more equitable income allocation and general welfare provision through geographically balanced growth.

A generation later, when Chiang Kai-shek faced the prospect of implementing Sun's program, he assumed essentially the same postures. He reaffirmed the role of the state and the necessities of land reform and income and welfare equity. He spoke of foreign investment and international cooperation in the development of China. And he advocated a decentralization of industrial development to ensure that "industry [would] be distributed equally," bringing "cities and rural districts . . . into equilibrium."[10]

---

7. Sun, *International Development,* pp. 297, 300, 310, 333; "Cheng chien chih piao-shih" [The expression of political opinion], *KFCC* 2: 303.

8. Sun, *International Development,* pp. 129-130, 132, 138, 182, 197, 276, 306; *SMCI,* pp. 205-210.

9. See Sun, *International Development,* pp. 144, 147.

10. Chiang, "Chapters," *Supplement,* p. 287.

Thus, both Sun and Chiang conceived China's development as proceeding through intensive involvement in the worldwide market economy. Both maintained that China's development would be inspired and directed by the interventionist state controlling private capital and foreign trade through a comprehensive policy that would ensure balanced growth, decentralized industry, substantial equality in income distribution, opportunities for private economic initiative, and competitiveness in the international market. In the process expanded welfare and educational facilities would provide social services that would extend longevity, enhance public health, and make literacy universal.[11]

This was the outline of a plan of industrialization that the Kuomintang brought with it to Taiwan. By 1953 the commitment to the creation of a "model province" involved all the energies of the government of the Republic of China. By that time it was evident that a return to the mainland, lost to the forces of Mao Tse-tung, would be delayed indefinitely. The only option that remained to the heirs of Sun Yat-sen was to proceed with the development of a min-sheng society on the remnant of the nation that remained under Kuomintang control. Land reform had already been substantially accomplished; now, a policy of industrialization through import substitution was initiated.

To initiate its program of import substitution the political authorities of the Republic of China needed to reduce the rate of inflation that had critically destabilized Taiwan's economy. Between October 1945 and June 1949 currency and currency substitutes on the island had expanded by about 600 percent. By 1948 prices were rising at an annual rate of 1,145 percent. The growth of the money supply and the rate of inflation began to slow down in 1951-1952 at least in part as a consequence of massive aid from the United States. That aid provided for importing essential foodstuffs and intermediate agricultural and capital goods while mandating, as a condition of aid, that substantial amounts of national currency be withdrawn from circulation as "counterpart funds." That condition conjoined with stringent fiscal policies produced a rapid decline in the rate of inflation from (approximately) 3,400 percent in 1949, to 500 percent in 1950, to 57 percent in 1951, to 17 percent in 1952, and to 4.5 percent in 1953.[12]

---

11. See ibid., pp. 321, 242, 272, 318.
12. Kowie Chang, ed., *Economic Development in Taiwan* (Taipei: Cheng Chung Publisher, 1968), pp. 390-392, 473-474, and p. 477, Table 8-8; Ching-yuan Lin, *Industrialization in Taiwan, 1946-72* (New York: Praeger, 1973), pp. 33-48; Henry Y. Wan, Jr., "Manpower, Industrialization and Export-led Growth—the Taiwan Experience," in *Growth, Distribution, and Social Change: Essays on the Economy of the Republic of China,* ed. Yuan-li Wu and Kung-chia Yeh (Baltimore: University of Maryland School of Law, 1978), pp. 139-140.

In September 1953 the Economic Stabilization Board and its subsidiary, the Industrial Development Commission, were created. The creation of such cabinet level agencies provided the centralized parastate machinery for administering the program of development. Such agencies faced a tangle of problems including a population increasing at more than 3 percent per annum—increasing Taiwan's population by nearly three million between 1946 and 1953—and a sizable trade deficit that threatened the island's foreign reserves. With the loss of markets in Japan and mainland China and the high demand for food and nondurable consumer goods on the island, a variety of small-scale consumer goods and simple manufacturing industries had sprung up on Taiwan between 1946 and 1950. Without import controls and the extensive use of foreign-exchange restraints, such industries, characterized by poor quality goods and high production costs, would have rapidly succumbed to foreign competition.

To shelter those industries the authorities on Taiwan, as early as 1949, initiated a program of foreign exchange controls that required exporters and other recipients of foreign exchange to sell foreign-exchange earnings to the state bank at manipulated official rates. By 1951 the ROC, employing such devices, entered into a period of stringent foreign-exchange and import controls. Goods imported by the public sector and goods necessary for domestic production were provided a favorable exchange rate, while other imported goods, particularly finished consumer commodities, suffered a corresponding discount. In effect, through a system of multiple exchange rates, the state blocked selected imports and helped underwrite the development of import-substituting industries such as those producing chemicals, chemical fertilizers, and petrochemical goods. Throughout the 1950s a favored rate on foreign exchange afforded the privileged infant industries a premium and penalized the importers of finished consumer goods.[13]

By the early 1950s an increasing number of commodities were removed from the list of permissible imports and constrained by controls. By 1955 a whole range of consumer goods such as cotton and woolen yarn and man-made fibers were placed under control. The import of products such as leather and leather manufactures, cement, chemical fertilizers, soap, paper, tin plate, sewing machines, bicycles, and motorcycles was "temporarily suspended" or "controlled" by the trade control agencies. Such discretionary controls over imports provided a major instrument of infant industry protection and promotion. Together with the land reform legislation and income redistribution, foreign-exchange and import controls directed massive capital flows into the industrializing sector of the island's economy. The

---

13. Yuan-li Yu and Kung-chia Yeh, "Taiwan's External Economic Relations," in ibid., pp. 179-180.

foreign exchange and import constraints together with the income redistribution that attended land reform produced terms of trade and a price structure that favored the new import-substituting industries. As a consequence, the prices of nondurable consumer goods, such as textiles, rose sharply, only to fall as the domestic production of textiles expanded in response to the incentives provided by a protected market. Under such circumstances, by 1954 domestic production supplied an estimated 77 percent of manufactured domestic requirements, primarily in the consumer goods subsectors such as textiles and apparel, wood products and furniture, leather manufactures, and printing. In comparison, in 1937 imported goods accounted for more than 70 percent of Taiwan's apparent domestic consumption of manufactured goods. Protection had reduced Taiwan's high dependency on imports not only for nonfood manufacturing, but for most of the remaining subsectors. In terms of the sources of demand for the nascent industries, the substitution of actual and potential imports is estimated to have provided as much as 91 percent of the effective market demand and to have been responsible for the more than 229 percent increase in net value added in nonfood manufacturing between the last year of peak prewar production and 1954.[14]

The first four-year plan, which covered the period between 1953 and 1956, was calculated to stabilize the economy, increase domestic manufacturing production, reduce import dependency, and improve the island's balance of payments position. It was not comprehensive. The plan proposed projects and provided cues to investors and entrepreneurs. The government, although having in its service sufficient economic planners, did not produce detailed plans for development but permitted market influences to guide investments and enterprise.[15] The plan provided for the "centralized control" alluded to by Sun but allowed "liberal laws" to permit private individuals to respond to market signals in their undertakings. It provided "perspective," not prescription.[16] The plan was intended to allow private and foreign investors to make decisions that would be compatible with government policy. In such a situation, the public sector authorities would act as general planners and as suppliers and coordinators of key public goods—transportation and energy. Through a series of incentives and disincentives, legislative controls and financial policies, they affected intersectoral capital flows from agriculture to the industrializing sector, subsidized domestic plants, and supplied credit at predictable and reasonable rates.

---

14. Lin, *Industrialization in Taiwan,* chap. 4; Samuel P. S. Ho, *Economic Development of Taiwan* (New Haven: Yale University Press, 1978), pp. 187-188.

15. Neil Jacoby, *U.S. Aid to Taiwan* (New York: Praeger, 1966),p. 244.

16. Wanyong Kuo, "Economic Planning in Taiwan," in *Agriculture's Place,* pp. 245-251.

Employing such mechanisms to direct a mixed economy, state planning necessarily remained flexible and regularly subject to revision. As long as fixed capital formation and enterprise depend on initiatives taken by private investors, indicative—as distinct from prescriptive—planning would be characterized by considerable variability in goal attainment. Thus in the first four-year plan only agricultural and infrastructural investment reached their goals (97.2 percent and 105.9 percent, respectively). Manufacturing and electric power generation achieved only 71.4 percent and 84.0 percent of their goals. Mining attained only 32.0 percent of its investment target.[17] Similar variability in subsectoral performance characterized the first and every subsequent four-year macroplan.

Although performance varied, the share of manufacturing of the gross domestic product rose from 16 percent in 1952 to 22 percent in 1959, growing significantly faster during the first two four-year plans than did other sectors of the Taiwanese economy.[18] Foreign-exchange incentives, import constraints, tariff controls, and an insulated domestic market stimulated a rapid growth in food processing, textiles, wearing apparel, and leather goods industries followed by the chemical and chemical products, petroleum, coal, rubber, and plastic goods industries. Related manufacturing industries, such as nonmetallic mineral products, basic metal products, fabricated metal products and machinery, increased their contribution to gross domestic production from 8 percent in 1952 to 17 percent in 1959.[19] Given the import-substitution goals, the mix of exchange controls, multiple exchange rates, import licensing, and protective tariffs, the share of consumer goods in total imports fell from 19.8 percent in 1952 to 6.6 percent in 1957, and imports of consumer goods as a percentage of total domestic supply of consumer goods dropped to only 5 percent by the end of the 1950s.[20]

While fostering domestic industrial production, direct government actions were critical in supplying large-scale overhead capital to the emerging industries. There was a concerted effort to expand the transportation infrastructure. Within a short period railway development provided road and rail density measured in meters per square kilometer second only to that of

17. Chang, *Economic Development in Taiwan,* p. 681, Table 11-2.
18. Republic of China, Directorate General of Budget, Accounting and Statistics, *Statistical Yearbook of the Republic of China 1975* (Taipei: Directorate General of Budget, Accounting and Statistics, 1975), p. 191.
19. Ching-yuan Lin, "Industrial Development and Changes in the Structure of Foreign Trade," *International Monetary Fund Staff Papers,* no. 15 (Washington, D.C.: IMF, July 1968), pp. 290-321.
20. Gustav Ranis, "Industrial Development," in *Economic Growth and Structural Change in Taiwan,* ed. Walter Galenson (Ithaca, N.Y.: Cornell University Press, 1979), p. 211.

Japan. Power generation projects were undertaken (supported as we have seen with U.S. project aid allocations) that allowed capacity to remain well ahead of demand at realistic pricing levels. The authorities also established several industry-oriented technology and investment institutes (such as the China Productivity and Trade Center, the Food Industry Research and Development Institute, and the Industrial Development and Investment Center) to afford management training, marketing information, and technical assistance as well as credit for industrial entrepreneurs.

In effect, flexible macroeconomic planning, facilitated by the policy and fiscal mechanisms to which allusion has been made, redirected foreign-exchange resources used in infrastructural construction, sheltering and expanding existing industry and providing profit incentives to the relatively inexperienced domestic, modernizing, entrepreneurial class. With agricultural expansion providing most of the domestic capital needed to finance nonagricultural development, the first four-year plan laid the foundation for subsequent industrial growth. Between 1949 and 1954 manufacturing production increased at an average annual rate of 22 percent. The rehabilitation of plants damaged during the war provided some of its substance, but the policy of import substitution and sheltered growth exerted considerable influence on its pace and character.[21] The first four-year plan shifted the emphasis from security and economic stabilization, which had prevailed from 1949 to 1953, to development. Heavy commitments were made to infrastructural, human resources, agriculture production, and industrial projects.[22]

Irrespective of its apparent success, much discussion has collected around the advisability of the Kuomintang's four-year plan of infant industry protection. The question is whether a policy emphasizing insulated home markets was misplaced and whether Taiwanese development might not have been more effectively sustained by export promotion instead.[23] For less developed countries (LDCs) facing circumstances similar to those with which Taiwan was compelled to deal, the question is significant. Several considerations seem critical in assessing alternative developmental options for LDCs,

21. Alice Amsden, "Taiwan's Economic History," *Modern China* 5, no. 3 (July 1979): 364-365; Hsing Mo-huan, John H. Power, and Gerardo P. Sicat, *Taiwan and the Philippines: Industrialization and Trade Policies* (London: Oxford University Press, 1970), pp. 238-266.
22. See Council for International Economic Cooperation and Development, *Taiwan Statistical Data Book* (Taipei: Council for International Economic Cooperation and Development, 1971), pp. 147, 149-150, and Tables 11-5 and 11-7.
23. See Maurice Scott, "Foreign Trade," in *Economic Growth and Structural Change in Taiwan*, pp. 378-381; Lin, *Industrialization in Taiwan*, pp. 162-165; Wu and Yeh, "Taiwan's External Economic Relations," in *Growth, Distribution and Social Change*, pp. 176-182.

but all must operate under comparable constraints. When LDCs undertake programs of development, almost all of them are producers and exporters of primary goods. Almost all have some history of colonial or quasi-colonial dependency. During the dependent period, primary goods exports were allowed free access into the metropolitan countries because export activities were dominated by entrepreneurs from the metropolitan country itself—entrepreneurs to whom the major share of profits accrued. When the colonial or dependent relationship was severed, the newly independent LDCs lost their assured export markets but remained burdened by domestic consumer demands. A new nation, possessed of a government with little legitimacy, faced the task of satisfying domestic needs without any assurance that it would be able to maintain primary goods exports at a level that would provide the foreign exchange to pay for consumer commodities imports.

To ensure themselves some reasonable measure of internal political stability, such new nations are compelled to meet at least minimal subsistence requirements for their populations. With decolonization and the loss of assured markets, many LDCs incurred escalating external debts to meet existing domestic demand. Under such circumstances, existing demand offers the option of sheltered industrialization and import substitution. Pursuit of such an option makes it possible to deal effectively with foreign exchange shortfall and also to escape from the less dynamic economic role of primary goods production and export, a role which had afforded the dependent areas little opportunity for rapid capital accumulation or accelerated economic growth. Decolonization created the possibility of both. Any LDC so circumstanced might choose sheltered, import-substitution-led growth to provide for the minimum needs of its population, foster political stability, solve its foreign exchange problem, and allow for economic development.

Like many other LDCs, Taiwan, after retrocession to the Republic of China and isolation from the mainland, made responses very much like those of similarly circumstanced economies. The authorities on Taiwan sought to transfer much of the surplus produced by the primary goods sector, which under colonial dependency would have gone to the metropole, to the modernizing and industrializing sectors of the economy. Intersectoral capital flow thus fueled domestic production to satisfy existing demand and underwrite infrastructural development.

Taiwan, cut off from its traditional markets, had to contend with a rapidly increasing population, which generated a critical demand for consumer goods that Japan had hitherto provided. Taiwan could hardly depend on the continued export of rice, sugar, bananas, pineapples, and tea to earn its foreign reserves for the purchase of foreign consumer goods, since neither Japan nor mainland China could serve as an assured market for such products. Furthermore, the world demand for such goods was relatively inelastic. Any restoration of prewar productivity could not assure increased foreign exchange earnings rapidly enough to satisfy the growing domestic needs of Taiwan's burgeoning population. Moreover, the high degree of commodity concentration required by such a course would be risky without a secure market. Finally, given the political circumstances, and the real and persistent threat of military attack or subversion initiated by its enemies on the Chinese mainland, the Kuomintang regime would have been threatened by any instability in the economy and the attendant disaffection of the population.

Taiwan could have attempted (as did Hong Kong) immediately to develop industries for export and to promote export-led industrial development. The foreign exchange earned in export trade would then have been used to supply domestic consumer demand and finance industrial expansion. Given Taiwan's abundance of cheap labor, such a course had much to recommend it, but it would have required a massive inflow of foreign capital and foreign entrepreneurial skill to establish export-oriented industries. Given Taiwan's parlous political and international diplomatic circumstances, such an inflow was unlikely. Furthermore, such a program would have surrendered Taiwan's future development largely to foreign firms and foreign interests whose central preoccupation was profit sensitive and who were totally unresponsive to political or "historic" imperatives. For an enclave like Hong Kong such circumstances would be unobjectionable. Hong Kong has neither independent political life nor autonomous political aspirations. It has no sovereign future nor does it pretend to an historic mission. For a system that has political substance and conceives itself animated by a "sacred" responsibility, however, such an option would be singularly unappealing.

The Republic of China on Taiwan thus had strong, immediate, noneconomic motives for pursuing an initial policy of import substitution and sheltered industrial development. Most LDCs, with far less political inspiration, have chosen similar paths to industrialization and modernization. Most developing countries after the Second World War had chosen import substitution policies very similar to those undertaken on Taiwan even when the economics of comparative advantage would recommend policies of export-led growth with its consequent dependence on foreign investment and the employment of foreign managerial, scientific, and technical personnel. In rejecting such a course, most LDCs have been prepared to sacrifice immediate material advantage to purchase the noneconomic benefits of sovereign control over their own collective destinies. However difficult, such a choice involves a logic intuitively comprehensible to nationalists the world over.[24] This is particularly true when ideological convictions inspire the drive

24. See Harry G. Johnson, "A Theoretical Model of Economic Nationalism in New and Developing States," in *Economic Nationalism in Old and New States,* ed. Harry G. Johnson (London: George Allen & Unwin, 1968), pp. 1-3.

toward modernization and industrialization and involve essentially noneconomic goals such as "equitable" income and welfare distribution and the pursuit of "historic national interests."

The Republic of China on Taiwan shared many of the dispositional traits of other LDCs in the period following the Second World War. Those traits, including the commitment to nationalist aspirations common to almost all LDCs, and the developmental policies they implied had been anticipated by Sun Yat-sen more than a quarter of a century before. Such nationalist aspirations are sometimes inscrutable to Western economists, whose assessments are governed almost exclusively by short-run, cost-benefit accounting, but they remain determinate historic factors nonetheless. Given its aspirations, the Republic of China on Taiwan would hardly have been content with an entrepôt economy or one that did not offer the promise of sovereign independence, adequate defense capabilities, and the prospect of satisfying the nationalist and min-sheng goals of Sun Yat-sen. Without a domestic industry responsive to political influence, Taiwan's development would follow market signals to the conceivable detriment of ideological purpose. Too great a dependence on foreign capital and foreign expertise might well compromise the political and social character of development. The tutelary state would be compelled either to follow the lead of policies dictated by a market outside its control or to engage in regular and disabling conflict with foreign entrepreneurs who controlled the flow of capital and critical talents. The alienation of Taiwan's industries to foreign control might abort the nationalist and social policies of the Kuomintang and impair the controls of the tutelary state. Without substantial control of the economic base, the government could not assure that the policy goals of balanced growth, equitable income distribution, and political sovereignty could be attained.

Whatever the motives that inspired it and whatever the successes that attended it, the first four-year plan did not solve Taiwan's foreign exchange problems. The development of import substitution industries required large-scale importation of capital and raw materials. Manufacturing output on Taiwan doubled between 1952 and 1958, and real gross domestic product grew 7.1 percent per annum.[25] The Taiwan Production Board oversaw the rapid expansion of the textile industry and the increasing production of plastics, artificial fibre, glass, cement, fertilizer, plywood, and chemicals—all of which required the import of basic raw materials. As a consequence, the balance of payments remained heavily in deficit, with exports financing only about 60 percent of imports. The shortfall was made up by United States aid; but since the deficit showed no disposition to decline and since American aid could not be expected to last forever, some alternatives had to be sought.

25. See *Industry of Free China,* January 1955, p. 33.

That domestic industries, responding to indigenous demand, would ultimately by profitable enough to supply the requisite funds was unlikely. Domestic markets were too small to provide for the necessary economies of scale. By 1956 there was evidence of domestic market saturation.[26] By the end of the 1950s "many plants producing simple manufactures, such as wollen textiles, plywood, paper, rubber goods, soap, iron rods and bars, insulated wires, sewing machines, and electric fans, were operating at only 40 percent to 70 percent of capacity."[27] Consequently, private sector gross investment in fixed capital formation fell from 56 percent in 1954 to 41 percent in 1958.[28] "As to the lack of investment," K. T. Li explained at the time, "it is because productive sectors with handsome returns but involving little risk have beeen developed more or less to a saturation point and can no longer absorb more investment."[29] The satisfaction of effective demand in the internal market produced a decline in the rate of overall manufacturing growth, a reduction of investment, a substantial price decline in nondurable consumer goods, and increasing competition among producers.

At the close of the first four-year plan Taiwan was clearly approaching a critical stage in its economic development. Unlike the governments of most other LDCs similarly circumstanced, the authorities on Taiwan decided that a change in course would be required to reduce foreign indebtedness and dependency on American aid, sustain overall growth, and extend and intensify industrialization. The second four-year plan (1957-1960), drawn up at the close of 1956, already contained the elements of redirection. There was a clear commitment to the expansion of exports in the effort to increase domestic private investment and reduce foreign indebtedness. The leadership on Taiwan recognized that "easy" import substitution had come to an end and that the only alternative that remained, if industrial development was to continue, was export-led growth.

For an economy like Taiwan's such an option could only produce far-reaching reassessment of existing policy. The first stage of growth had been inspired by a programmatic strategy embodied in the writings of Sun and reflected in the doctrinal commitments expressed by Chiang Kai-shek. That strategy and those commitments, however, presupposed continental China as

---

26. See the speech of P. Kiang, then Minister of Economic Affairs, in *Industry of Free China,* October 1956, pp. 2-3.
27. Kuo-shu Liang and T. H. Lee, "Taiwan," in *The Economic Development of East and Southeast Asia,* ed. Shinichi Ichimura (Honolulu: East-West Center Press, 1975), p. 295.
28. Chang, *Economic Development in Taiwan,* p. 80, Table 2-31.
29. K. T. Li, "A Review of the Economic Situation in Taiwan in 1958," *Industry of Free China,* March 1959, p. 8.

the economic base for Chinese economic modernization and industrialization. Given that assumption, development would have been predicated on a generous resource base, a vast pool of relatively cheap labor, and a large internal market. The situation on Taiwan was radically different. Taiwan had a restricted market, very few mineral and fossil fuel resources, and severely limited agricultural endowments. Its irregular rainfall allowed little hydroelectric potential. The only competitive advantage enjoyed by the Taiwanese economy was its abundance of labor, upgraded by extensive educational facilities that had been established during the first four-year plan. Employing that labor in industry could only take the form of adding value to imported, rather than domestically available, materials.

Sun Yat-sen had been insistent upon the international competitive advantage of low labor costs in the development of the Chinese economy. To exploit that endowment, he counseled Chinese programmers to support economic development and industrialization by selecting "the most remunerative field . . . in order to attract foreign capital." To exploit its comparative advantages, China would have to weigh opportunity costs judiciously ("the most suitable positions must be chosen") and pursue the "lines of least resistance" in putting together specific programs.[30] Given Taiwan's lack of natural resources, after the stage of sheltered growth had been concluded, only its abundant supply of efficient labor could fuel subsequent growth. Without mainland China's resources and internal market as its base, Taiwan's development was obliged to shift into export-led modalities.

Because of Taiwan's limited choices in seeking "the most remunerative field," any effort to promote development through export-led growth involved several preconditions. In the first place, competitiveness of Taiwanese exports on the world market required that local manufacturers have access to imported raw materials, components, and capital equipment at no more than world prices. Since all the necessary raw materials and productive components would have to be imported, such materials could account for 65 to 70 percent of selling values. This meant that any import duties, commodity taxes, or surcharges might make exports noncompetitive on the world market. In 1954, for example, the commodity tax applied to domestically produced and imported goods was levied at 15 percent on cotton yarn and rayon staple fiber yarn, 20 percent on artificial filament yarn, and 30 percent on woolen yarn. Such taxes alone were enough to make such textile goods noncompetitive in international trade.[31] Only rebating or eliminating such taxes on goods for export could restore their profitability and competitiveness on the world market. Moreover, even if imported raw materials

30. Sun, *International Development*, pp. 297, 300, 303, 310, 333.
31. Scott, "Foreign Trade," p. 321.

could be obtained at no more than world prices, only efficient labor could provide the margin that would make exports capable of returning enough to reduce foreign indebtedness.

To attempt to satisfy these preconditions of export-led growth, the Kuomintang authorities, as early as 1955, worked for the passage of the "Regulations for Rebate of Taxes on Export Products" that would rebate the taxes on imported inputs that threatened to reduce or eliminate the margin between input costs and price that made export goods profitable. Secondly, there were moves to devalue the national currency so that certain inputs (chiefly wages) would be reduced relative to international costs. Moreover, given government control of the staples in the national diet, food costs could be kept relatively low, further reducing the wage costs for potential exporters.

In 1957 the state Bank of Taiwan introduced low-cost loans as incentives to exports (at 6 percent per annum payable in foreign exchange). Government export insurance was provided, direct subsidies were offered to promising export industries, and export marketing research was made available by government institutes. In 1958 a major foreign exchange reform was undertaken, dismantling the multiple exchange rate system that had prevailed during the phase of import substitution.[32] In 1959 tariff rates for a number of finished goods and their major imported components were reduced. Import controls, mechanisms employed to protect infant industry development, were relaxed, and more and more items were removed from control.

During the second four-year plan modifications in the foreign exchange, commodity tax, import controls, fiscal, and monetary policies added up to a major change in the government's program, which shifted from an essentially domestic raw materials and agriculture-based to an imported raw materials and labor-based pattern of development and industrialization. After 1960 Taiwan's development was to be sustained by exploiting its economic advantages—a relatively abundant supply of labor combined with growing entrepreneurial skills—to penetrate world markets with the products of its labor-intensive consumer goods industries.

At the end of the second four-year plan an Accelerated Economic Development Program was formulated, which together with a 19-Point Financial and Economic Reform Program was designed to improve the climate for private investment, stimulate the growth of private-sector industry, and improve the foreign exchange situation. An Industrial Development and Investment Center was instituted, and in 1960 the Statute for Encouragement of Investment was promulgated, providing the legislative basis for

---

32. Lin, *Industrialization in Taiwan,* pp. 74-76.

development during the third four-year plan (1961-1964).

During this period net domestic savings rose from 18 percent of gross capital formation in 1959 to 60.6 percent in 1965. The ratio of foreign to indigenous capital declined from 46 percent in 1959 to 16 percent in 1965.[33] The investment that accrued to the modern sectors of the economy resulted in major structural changes. The share of manufactured products to total exports averaged 41 percent between 1959 and 1965, compared with the average of 12 percent between 1952 and 1958.[34] Such import-substitution products developed during the period of sheltered growth as processed foodstuffs, beverages, tobacco, textiles, leather, wood items, paper and related products constituted 58 percent of the total increase in exports between 1959 and 1965. Reflecting domestic factor endowments, the first period of export-led growth involved two major industrial subsectors: processed food production and textiles—both of which were labor-intensive. The food processing industry was more capital-intensive than the average Taiwanese industry, but the accomplishments of the island's agricultural sector made the export of agricultural products particularly profitable. Nonetheless, labor-intensive consumer and consumer-oriented goods dominated Taiwanese exports during the first phase of "outward directed" economic growth. By the mid-1960s there was a shift to more capital- and technological-intensive subsectors of the intermediate goods industries. The emphasis began to shift from cement and paper to chemicals and petroleum products. Durable consumer goods industries began to expand in the mid-1960s with machinery and electrical machinery manufacture.

Because of these changes, the industrial sector of the economy expanded at a 20 percent annual rate compared to the 10 percent annual rate of the 1950s. Attending this growth was a proliferation of state institutions to service the special needs of industrial subsectors. The Industrial Development and Investment Center was expanded, and a Medium and Small-Sized Enterprises Assistance Working Group was formed to assist small-scale enterprises in obtaining credit, developing managerial and marketing skills, and gaining access to the latest manufacturing techniques. A Metal Industries Development Center was devoted to providing similar assistance to the metallurgical industries, and the Union Industrial Research Institute conducted research and provided information on organic, inorganic, petroleum, and agricultural chemicals, metallurgy, and construction materials.

During the fourth and fifth four-year plans (1965-1968, 1969-1972) the economy grew rapidly. Per capita income growth rates more than

---

33. Chang, *Economic Development in Taiwan,* p. 680, Table 11-1.
34. Republic of China, Economic Planning Council, *Taiwan Statistical Data Book* (Taipei: Economic Planning Council, 1976), p. 182.

doubled. The industrial sector grew dramatically. Between 1962 and 1972 chemical, basic metal, and machinery products increased their net contribution to the gross domestic product from about 25 percent to about 50 percent.[35] Textile and apparel production held their own, relative to aggregate manufacturing output. At the same time the agricultural sector continued its dynamic growth, without which the supply of labor at competitive costs would have been threatened and increased costs would have eroded the relative advantages enjoyed by Taiwanese exports on the world market. In fact, Taiwan's successful economic development would have been seriously compromised had it not been for the generally balanced growth of agriculture and industry.

Such balanced growth would not have been possible if infrastructural development had not taken place during the preliminary phases of postwar restabilization and restoration. As we have seen, both Sun and Chiang had emphasized the importance of infrastructural articulation in any program of economic growth and modernization. Given the network of roads and rails, along with ready access to energy supplies at realistic price levels, both industry and agriculture could benefit from technological innovation. More than that, the availability of such an infrastructure permitted Taiwanese industry to be dispersed. Gustav Ranis credits that regional character of manufacturing a "key" to Taiwan's successful growth and industrialization.[36]

Perhaps the most interesting features of the process of industrialization on Taiwan turn on the creative implementation of Sun's policies by the planning agencies of the government. The various elements of his program were combined in a fashion that permitted their interpenetration and mutual support.

Industrial development on Taiwan did not produce disabling urbanization with its high social overhead costs and population dislocations characteristic of the same process in other LDCs largely because the proportion of industrial establishments situated in the five largest cities on the island did not substantially change in the twenty years between 1951 and 1970. The proportion of persons employed in manufacturing occupations in the cities, in fact, actually declined from 43 percent to 37 percent between 1956 and 1966 and remained virtually unchanged into the 1970s because industrial establishments could employ part-time, seasonal, and commuter rural labor without depopulating the countryside. Such an accomplishment was contingent on the availability of rapid and efficient transportation as well as the provision of energy to "ruralized" manufacturing establishments at competitive costs. Without the antecedent development of a communications, trans-

35. Wan, "Manpower, Industrialization and Export-led Growth," p. 144, Table 3.
36. Ranis, "Industrial Development," p. 222.

portation, and energy supply infrastructure the ruralization of industry would have been impossible.

Because rural labor could be so employed, farm households could enjoy the wage benefits available in the industrial sector; this situation tended to equalize family income between the rural and urban areas. By 1960 less than 50 percent of Taiwan's farm families were fully engaged in farming; 31 percent were employed at least part-time in the nonagricultural sector and 20 percent considered agriculture only as a supplementary source of income. In 1964 nonagricultural income made up 32 percent of total farm family income, while by 1972 more than 50 percent of farm household income originated in the nonagricultural sectors.[37] The supplement to farm household incomes which derived from participation in the nonagricultural sectors not only provided more income equity, but also allowed a steady increase in the effective demand that would fuel continued industrial growth throughout the 1960s.

The political authorities on Taiwan fostered all of this by their efforts to reduce any advantages industry might enjoy by concentrating in urban settings. Rural electrification and equality between urban and rural power rates reduced any economic incentives that might have skewed the pattern of industrial development on the island. The government invested in rural industrial estates, organizing the essential physical overheads that would make such rural locations attractive to private industry. By 1966 the government had established seventeen such rural industrial areas, providing the necessary communications, transportation, and overhead adjuncts, and then selling plots to private investors.

The decentralization of industrial development on Taiwan afforded manufacturing establishments direct access to the economy's major asset: abundant and efficient labor. That the labor force was efficient was at least in part the consequence of the educational program initiated almost immediately upon the political stabilization of the island. The supply of rural labor readily trainable into semiskilled workers was critical to Taiwan's rapid industrialization.[38] Manpower development programs in terms of educational expenditures have involved at least one-quarter of the total provincial budget on Taiwan since 1952 (compared to the 6.42 percent of total provided in the best years of the Japanese administration).[39] During the period of labor-

37. Ho, *Economic Development of Taiwan,* p. 254; Ranis, "Industrial Development," pp. 228-229. See also Shih Chien-sheng, "The Contribution of Education to Economic Development in Taiwan," speech before the Conference on Population and Economic Development in Taiwan (Taipei: Institute of Economics, 1976); and Pien Yü-yüan, *Kung-yeh-hua yü nung chia-shou te fen-p'ei* [Industrialization and agricultural income distribution], (Taipei: Academia Sinica, 1979).
38. Wan, "Manpower, Industrialization and Export-led Growth," pp. 161-163.
39. Chang, *Economic Development in Taiwan,* p. 631, Table 10-3; Republic of China,

intensive production that extended through the 1960s into the early 1970s the textile, chemical, and telecommunications assembly industries depended largely on semiskilled workers produced in large numbers by the educational campaigns of the 1950s. By 1968 the effort to upgrade the labor force prompted the extension of publicly financed education from six to nine years. By 1970 economic development on Taiwan was unique in the extent to which attention was devoted to mass education. Even though Taiwan is a developing nation, its educational system more closely approximates that of a developed nation like the United Kingdom than those of the "third world."[40]

Sun's emphasis on mass education, insisted upon as early as his reform proposals to Li Hung-chang in 1894 and repeated throughout his life, had become part of the developmental ideology of the Kuomintang. In 1953, when Chiang Kai-shek wrote the two concluding chapters to Sun's incomplete lectures on the *San-min chu-i,* he devoted considerable space to the necessity for an educational program that would train students to enter the nation's job market.[41] The mass literacy campaigns of the 1950s and the subsequent sustained emphasis on education provided the semiskilled and skilled manpower essential to Taiwan's economic growth and development.

All the elements insisted upon by Sun—a requisite infrastructure, decentralization of industry, and mass education—had been put together by the authorities on Taiwan in a fashion that permitted sustained agricultural and industrial growth while maintaining relative family income equity. Long familiar with the economic programs of min-sheng, the administrators and planners of Taiwan's development had affected programs that had changed Taiwan's economic system from a traditional one to one that had become increasingly modern while satisfying the essentials of Sun's social goals.

Between 1953 and 1974 industrial production on Taiwan increased at an annual average rate of 14.4 percent. Disaggregated, the rate of growth averaged 12.2 percent during the first half of the period, then accelerated to 17.2 percent during the subsequent half. Industrial production as a proportion of net domestic product rose from 11 percent to 31 percent of the total. By 1973 domestic savings as a percent of national income had increased to 32.3 percent, higher than the percentages in any other economy in Asia, and higher than that in most of the world's economies. By 1974 almost 84

Council for Economic Planning and Development, *Social Welfare Indicators, Republic of China 1979* (Taipei: Council for Economic Planning and Development, September 1979), p. 68, Table A-6.

40. See Republic of China, Taipei Ministry of Education, *Educational Statistics of the Republic of China* (Taipei: Taipei Ministry of Education, 1979); United Nations, *United Nations' Statistical Yearbook 1979* (New York: United Nations, 1979); Ralph N. Clough, *Island China* (Cambridge: Harvard University Press, 1978), p. 71, n. 9.

41. Chiang, "Chapters," pp. 258, 261, 270, 277.

percent of Taiwan's exports were industrial products. The composition of Taiwan's imports changed until by 1975 consumption goods amounted to only 7 percent of total imports, and raw materials and capital goods had increased to 61 and 32 percent respectively. Export volume accelerated throughout this period, increasing at an average annual rate of 23 percent from 1960 to 1973. Because exports rose faster than imports (which grew at a rate of 18 percent annually during this period) the trade balance improved, and by 1964 exports financed about 100 percent of imports of goods and services. In 1963 the United States decided to terminate aid to Taiwan in 1965; it was estimated that the Republic of China on Taiwan, without aid supports, could sustain a rate of growth of about 6 to 7 percent per annum. In fact, the rate of growth from 1964 through 1972 was about 10 percent. Given these circumstances, after 1964 the government on Taiwan had little reason to concern itself about the balance of payments. Foreign loans and long-term foreign capital inflow were used to build up fixed assets and foreign exchange reserves, with exports of Taiwanese goods and services financing about 99 percent of imports.

By the early 1970s the Republic of China on Taiwan was recognized as a "hero" of development and industrialization.[42] Few LDCs had recorded such a remarkable history of stable, balanced growth. For two decades Taiwan's growth exceeded the target set by the United Nations Decade of Development. The rate of growth in national income (valued in U.S. dollars) was 6.2 percent per annum during the first four-year plan (1953-1956), accelerating to 6.5 percent between 1957 and 1960, and to 9.7 percent between 1961 and 1970. During the same period per capita income rose from 2.6 percent per annum during the first four-year plan, to 3.1 percent between 1957 and 1960, and 6.5 percent between 1961 and 1970. In two decades a major structural change in the economy had occurred. Between 1953 and 1968 the share of agricultural output in the nation's gross domestic production fell from 41.8 percent to 24.4 percent, and the share of industry rose from 11.6 to 21.2 percent. Taiwan was no longer a traditional agrarian country. By 1970 Taiwan was a "semideveloped" country on its way to economic maturation.

Much of that impressive performance had been prefigured in the programmatic plans left to the Kuomintang by Sun Yat-sen. The recognition that the economic development of China required a transfer of capital from the less dynamic agricultural to the more dynamic industrial sectors was already explicit by about 1905. All the intellectuals who collected around Sun's revolutionary standard recognized that domestic capital formation

---

42. See Herman Kahn, *World Economic Development 1979 and Beyond* (Boulder, Colo.: Westview Press, 1979), chap. 6.

required intersectoral capital flows. The program of "equalization of land rights," with government acquisition of unearned increment, was one device for accomplishing such transfers. It was also the device that was politically least objectionable. For at least that reason, it was given prominent place in a developmental program that came to include rent reform and land distribution as well. The entire program anticipated a rapid growth in agricultural production under the spur of rent reduction and land redistribution and a consequent transfer of capital from the traditional to the modern sector. The accumulation of domestic capital would be supplemented by foreign capital and foreign technical assistance. Exploiting the country's natural endowments and sheltered by a system of import controls, the infant industries of China would take root. Using its low-cost labor, China could compete effectively in the world market, earning enough foreign exchange to reduce foreign indebtedness while building up its domestic capital.[43] The subsequent growth of industry would be decentralized along the communications, transportation, and energy supply network provided by initial heavy investment.

All of this was undertaken, as Sun had advocated, under the aegis of a tutelary state. Land reform and land redistribution were designed and implemented by the state. Executive and legislative government actions controlled the prices of domestic comestibles, raw materials, and intermediary inputs into the economy. Education and infrastructural development was initiated by government programs, while licensing, quotas, and tariffs controlled the island's international commerce. That Sun's plans were implemented on Taiwan rather than on mainland China obviously involved significant changes in emphasis, the need for alternative instrumentalities, and different assessments of opportunity costs. That Taiwan was nearly devoid of natural resources and had only a small real and potential domestic market for its industrial goods meant that exports would have to lead any expansion in the modern sector. But even under such circumstances, Sun's recognition that low-cost labor would be critical to China's development permitted a strategy of export-led growth based on labor-intensive commodity production. This would be supported by such direct state intervention as rebates, tax holidays, easy credit, government sponsored unified and joint marketing programs, as

43. Sun had always understood that China would have to expand its foreign trade to generate the foreign reserves necessary for accelerated development. He argued that China's pool of low-cost labor could provide agricultural and textile products for export. Such commodities would attract foreign investment because of their international competitive advantage. See Sun, *International Development*, pp. 129-130, 132, 138, 306; and *SMCI*, pp. 205-210. In a speech to the Nationalist Chinese Economic Commission in November 1945, Chiang Kai-shek reflected Sun's admonitions concerning the advantages of export trade based on low-cost labor. See Chiang, *T'sung-t'ung* 17: 33.

well as by state-established industrial estates and export processing zones. As Sun had anticipated, the state's role in the management of capital accumulation became central to the economic modernization and industrialization of the Republic of China.[44] Although the manufacturing production of the public sector declined from 56.2 percent of total output in 1952 to 22.4 percent in 1970,[45] that decline can hardly serve as an indicator of state involvement in the developmental history of Taiwan.

Government policy on Taiwan reflected Sun's injunction that "all matters that can be and are better carried out by private enterprise should be left to private hands which should be encouraged and fully protected by liberal laws."[46] That injunction, together with China's expected involvement in international trade and finance, implied an indicative planning policy reflected in the outlines provided regularly by the state. Under such circumstances planning provides a general guide to potential investors and entrepreneurs and a list of priorities for internal decision making. Such a plan is a flexible program that emphasizes a goal. The general population is provided insight into what is expected, foreign investors are reassured, and the entire economy is given a sense of mission and accomplishment.

44. Keith Griffin, "An Assessment of Development in Taiwan," *World Development* 1, no. 6 (June 1973): 31, Table 1.
45. Amsden, "Taiwan's Economic History," p. 366; Republic of China, Council for International Economic Cooperation and Development, *Taiwan Statistical Data Yearbook 1971* (Taipei: Council for International Economic Cooperation and Development, 1971), p. 56, Table 5-4.
46. Sun, *International Development,* p. 9.

IV

The Drive to Maturity

By the early 1970s the economy of Taiwan had outdistanced many of Sun Yat-sen's suggestions concerning the initial phases of development and industrialization. Nonetheless, some explicit constraints, suggestions, and admonitions continued to influence his heirs in their planning.

By the time the energy crisis settled on the world in 1972-1973, the Republic of China on Taiwan had one of the highest rates of economic growth and per capita income in the world's developing countries. At the same time there were signals that significant changes were taking place in the national economy. The fifth four-year plan (1969-1972), for example, had anticipated an annual increase in agricultural production of 4.4 percent. In fact, the actual increase averaged 2.2 percent. Beginning with 1968 the absolute numbers of workers in the agricultural labor force declined. With essentially full employment on Taiwan—unemployment having fallen below the level of ordinary, frictional joblessness—wage rates in the industrial sector began to outdistance returns for farm labor, prompting a net population shift from the agricultural to the industrial sector. In effect, by the early 1970s the Republic of China on Taiwan began to display some of the first signs of industrial maturity, with agriculture no longer playing a significant role in the process of growth. Agriculture had become a passive, sustaining sector of an otherwise developing economy.[1]

During the phase of sheltered growth, a substantial portion of industrial profits in Taiwan had originated in windfalls that resulted from government interventions calculated to channel agriculture-based surpluses into the industrial sector. By 1973 industrial production had been so well established that it could sustain a level of production that both provided the internal market with manufactured commodities and rendered Taiwan an exporting nation with one of the highest trade to gross domestic product ratios in the

---

1. See Walter P. Falcon, "Lessons and Issues in Taiwan's Development," in *Agriculture's Place in the Strategy of Development: The Taiwan Experience,* ed. T. H. Shen (Taipei: Joint Commission on Rural Reconstruction [JCRR], 1975), p. 279.

world. Almost half (49 percent) of Taiwan's gross domestic production, more and more of it nonagricultural in origin, was exported.[2] With the success of export-led growth, industrial profits grew out of entrepreneurial skills and product competitiveness in the international market rather than from the availability of agricultural surpluses. By 1973 industrial products dominated exports, constituting about 85 percent of the total. Among these products were many—electronic, chemical, machinery equipment, and instruments— that were developed primarily for export rather than as import substitutes. The electronics industry, for example, based almost entirely on imported intermediate goods, was almost entirely export-oriented from its inception. Between 1964 and 1973 its average annual growth was 40 percent. Almost from their commencement, the industrial sectors that part-produced or assembled transistor radios, phonographs, television sets, tape recorders, and calculators were largely based on foreign investment seeking cheap and dependable labor in "off-shore" facilities. Within-firm markets, in turn, absorbed more than 80 percent of the output.

As the labor force became more skilled and better educated, manufacturers began to produce goods requiring a high level of skill and technology. Thus by 1973 more sophisticated electrical machinery and apparatus made up 17.2 percent of Taiwan's total exports, indicating both a capacity for higher value-added production and a diversification of export commodities.[3] The production of such equipment, coupled with that of machinery, high-quality textiles, and apparel, and with automobile production and shipbuilding, showed the increasing industrialization of the economy and the increasing diversification and sophistication of the commodities produced.

As a result of this growth, real per capita income rose substantially throughout the decade, and gross saving in Taiwan increased from 12 percent in 1960 to almost 26 percent in 1970.[4] Given its profitability and expansion, the industrial sector absorbed labor at an annual rate of 9 percent at a time when the population rate of growth was falling from 3.8 percent annually in

2. See Republic of China, Directorate-General of Budget, Accounting and Statistics, *Monthly Bulletin of Statistics: The Republic of China* (Taipei: Directorate-General of Budget, Accounting and Statistics, 1977), 3, no. 1 (January 1977): 18. See also Taiwan Importers and Exporters Association, *Trade Development in Past Two Decades: Republic of China (1953-1972),* (Taipei: Taiwan Importers and Exporters Association, 1973).

3. See Kuo-shu Liang and Ching-ing Hou Liang, "Exports and Employment in Taiwan," *Conference on Population and Economic Development in Taiwan* (Taipei: Academia Sinica, 1976).

4. Gustav Ranis, "Industrial Development," in *Economic Growth and Structural Change in Taiwan,* ed. Walter Galenson (Ithaca, N.Y.: Cornell University Press, 1979), pp. 241-242.

the early 1950s to about 2 percent annually in the late 1960s.

The energy, monetary, and trade crises of 1972-1974 severely jolted this economy. The crises reversed the steady growth in per capita income, industrial production, and export surpluses that had come to characterize Taiwan's small, trade-oriented economy. The immediate effect of the oil crisis, for example, was a trade deficit of $1.3 billion in 1974. For the first time since 1970 Taiwan's balance of payments went into deficit. In 1975 both exports and imports declined for the first time since 1969. In 1974 wholesale prices rose by about 35 percent, while the consumer price index escalated by 47 percent. Prices of imports rose by an average of 55 percent.[5] Inflationary pressures were fueled by the growing labor shortage that triggered wage increases in manufacturing industries. In 1974 industrial production declined by 1.5 percent, and real per capita income fell by 3 percent.

In response, the government intervened to reduce the level of inflation and cool the economy. Credit was restricted and a number of energy conservation measures were introduced. By the end of 1974 prices had stabilized, and by mid-1975 economic indicators had once more begun to rise. Industrial production grew at a relatively modest 5.8 percent in 1975, but by 1976 full recovery had begun. The relatively rapid recovery evidenced the effectiveness of government policies as well as the maturity of the economic system.

The crisis highlighted some of the problems that had already begun to surface in the early 1970s. One of those problems was the declining productivity of agriculture. Another was the increasingly evident shortage of labor. A third was the economy's heavy dependence on foreign sources of intermediate capital goods (steel, machinery, and chemicals). Most of Taiwan's negative balance of trade with Japan was the consequence of such purchases. The dependence on foreign sources for fuel exacerbated the foreign exchange problem and today increasingly threatens Taiwan's trade balance. Finally, there was and is the problem of Taiwan's inevitable sensitivity to the instability of world trade. With its economy dependent on exports, any alteration in world trading conditions necessarily influences Taiwan's economic well-being. By 1975 the government had put together a six-year plan intended to address all these problems—and to move the economy along the path of increasing maturity.

As early as 1969 the government had formulated a "New Agricultural Policy" intended to maintain self-sufficiency in food production, provide equitable income rates for the agricultural sector, and allow for net labor outflow into the industrial labor pool.[6] Nonetheless, between 1968 and 1975

---

5. "Taiwan Economic Statistics," *Industry of Free China,* March 1974, p. 5.
6. T. H. Shen, "A New Agricultural Policy," in *Agriculture's Place,* pp. 38-56.

the growth of agricultural output steadily declined. The binding constraint was apparently the shortage of labor. During this period there was an absolute decline in the number of workers, in the total number of man-days worked, and in the man-days worked per average agricultural worker. The cultivated crop area and the multiple crop index shrank because of labor shortages, especially during peak seasons. Labor costs as a share in the total cost of agricultural production rose sharply, reflecting an increase in the daily wage of farm workers. To solve its agricultural and labor shortage problems Taiwan needed to supplant human labor with machinery—with all the related changes in the scale and structure of food production such mechanization entailed.

Making such a transition, however, would involve a number of problems—the most important of which turns on the small size of the average farm on Taiwan. Individually-owned farm units in Taiwan currently average about one hectare, while the minimum size for the cost-effective use of power tillers and other mechanical implements is about three hectares.[7] Because mechanical energy is indivisible, it tends to be underutilized on small holdings in terms of its total horsepower capacity, making its use cost inefficient. Unless the productive units were expanded, the use of mechanical energy would do little, if anything, to reduce costs, to free labor, and to increase yield.

Sun Yat-sen had left several guidelines concerning agriculture. He had been a firm advocate of mechanized farming. At the same time he advocated a policy of agricultural self-sufficiency for the nation, defended the private ownership of the soil, and insisted upon equitable income for agricultural producers.[8] A commitment to all these policies severely limited the options open to the planners on Taiwan. Clearly, any attempt to pursue an "American solution" to Taiwan's agricultural problems—thoroughly mechanizing farm production through economies of scale—was precluded. Such a strategy would displace millions of rural Taiwanese and would imply the alienation of their private holdings to allow for land consolidation. A "Japanese solution" seemed almost as unattractive. Japan had resolved its agricultural problem by "creating a nation of part-time farmers," one in which 80 percent of the nation's farmers earn substantial off-farm incomes to maintain their standard of living. While such a solution might gradually emerge from the present arrangements, continuing some trends that have characterized Taiwanese agriculture in the past, it would involve allowing

---

7. See T. H. Shen, "Taiwan's Family Farm During Transitional Economic Growth," mimeographed (Taipei: JCRR, 1976).
8. Sun Yat-sen, San-min chu-i (Taipei: China Publishing, n. d.), pp. 179, 188-189. Cited as SMCI.

specifically farm incomes to deteriorate relative to the wage scales available in the maturing industrial and service sectors. The relative decline in agricultural incomes would compel farm families to seek nonfarm sources of income more aggressively to supplement their declining fortunes.[9]

Neither alternative would satisfy the injunctions of Sun Yat-sen, the first because it would alienate farmers from their land and the second because it would necessarily abandon farm incomes to impersonal market forces. Moreover, the latter alternative, since it would probably not increase agricultural yield, would threaten Taiwan's agricultural self-sufficiency.

Taiwan's Council for Economic Planning and Development (the lineal descendent of earlier parastate agencies) has apparently settled on a third alternative: increasing the size of agricultural productive units by separating farm ownership from farm operation. To that end the authorities have sponsored programs of joint operations, joint management, and contract farming, and have promoted specialized production areas. All of these programs are intended to increase the size of farms in order to employ labor-saving machinery without alienating private owners.

Joint operations and management involve cooperative undertakings during land preparation, plowing, or harvesting that would permit groups of farmers to invest in and fully utilize expensive farm equipment. Under a joint operation program, a group of farmers, working a consolidated block of twenty or twenty-five hectares could jointly and efficiently operate power tillers and tractors. Joint management or contract farming involve some of the same features, allowing a number of small plots to be consolidated, thereby expanding the size of the land unit to be worked. Such arrangements also entail the employment of a manager or contract farmer who undertakes to use mechanical farm implements to work consolidated land, sharing the profits and losses with those who have surrendered at least part of their management prerogatives to him in the interests of efficiency and productivity. Under a program of specialized production areas all producers of specialized agricultural commodities (feed corn, mushrooms, and asparagus, for example) would cooperatively prepare their land and harvest, store, and market their crops. Such cooperation would allow economies of scale and the cost-efficient and labor-saving use of modern machinery.

The growing shortage of agricultural labor and the efforts to implement programs of land consolidation have accelerated the use of farm machinery in Taiwan. Thus between 1967 and 1975 the number of power tillers in use almost tripled from about 17,000 to about 45,500. In 1967 there were 479 tractors used on Taiwan; by 1975 there were 1,323. In 1967 there were no power threshers; by 1975 there were 27,558 in use. In 1967 there were no

---

9. Falcon, "Lessons and Issues in Taiwan's Development," pp. 281-23.

rice transplanters or rice combines employed on Taiwan, and in 1975 there were 2,481 of the first and 1,940 of the second in service.[10]

During the same period, to maintain equitable farm incomes in the face of rising costs the government abolished the rice-barter system and sharply increased the price at which it purchased rice. The first measure caused an immediate drop in the tax burden shouldered by farmers, the second an increase of 300 percent in the official price for rice—all of which improved the relative income position of farmers. After 1970 the government made the maintenance of farm incomes a major objective. Between 1966 and 1978 the ratio of per capita farm income to that of nonfarm income reflected that choice. In 1966 the ratio of farm to nonfarm per capita income was .65, dropping to .53 in 1973, rising to .64 in 1978.[11]

The stabilization of per capita farm incomes has been effected by a program of price support for rice production. Because of the overwhelming importance of rice as a cash crop, supporting its price is the closest approximation to a nonselective, income-support policy available to the government in the agricultural sector. Because of the inelasticity of demand, the cost incurred by that policy is a large rice surplus. Taiwan now produces about 2.5 million tons of rice annually, about 300,000 tons in excess of domestic demand. In addition, the steady rise in per capita incomes on Taiwan has caused a significant change in diet. More meat, milk, fish, and fruit are now eaten at the expense of rice. The result has been a rice storage of over one million tons in government granaries. Export of rice is unprofitable because price supports have made production costs relatively high. At the same time livestock feed and nonrice grains are imported at considerable foreign exchange expense.[12]

The shift from rice production to higher-valued crops such as nonrice grains, fruit, and livestock would involve rising costs of production that would significantly affect agricultural incomes. To address these problems, budgetary costs of the price support system for rice production, as well as the entailed storage costs, must be weighed against the commitment to stable farm incomes and self-sufficiency.

However these particular issues are resolved, the future for Taiwanese agriculture includes a program of land management that will free labor by having farmers work larger productive units that will allow for cost-effective mechanization. It is projected that this will generate an increase in agricultural yield from 1.5 to 2.5 percent annually. Greater mechanization will

---

10. Erik Thorbecke, "Agricultural Development," in *Economic Growth,* p. 149, Table 2.7.

11. See ibid., p. 194, n. 93; and *China Post,* November 1, 1979, p. 4.

12. See *China Post,* October 29, 1979, p. 2.

allow the continued migration of labor from the rural areas to the expanding industrial sector at a projected rate of 2.9 percent annually. Wage incentives in the modern sector will continue to attract rural youth, with 60 percent of farm family income originating in nonagricultural sources and the ratio of farm per capita income to nonfarm per capita income stabilizing at .70 by 1989.[13]

Maintaining farm incomes at that level, however, means that the predictable flow of labor from the agricultural to the industrial sector would be insufficient to maintain the labor-intensive system at present levels of growth. Already in the early 1970s planning personnel on Taiwan discussed the need to shift to a more mature industrial growth regime increasingly based on skilled labor, labor-saving technology, and capital deepening to offset the increasing labor shortage. While Taiwanese industry in 1975 remained labor-intensive by international standards, with more than 40 percent of its production originating in light industries, that 40 percent was down from more than 50 percent in 1966—evidence of a significant shift toward commodity production involving more skilled workers, labor-saving machinery, technological sophistication, and capital.[14]

The shift to more sophisticated machine production is calculated not only to maintain farm production and help resolve Taiwan's labor shortage, but to reduce its dependence on foreign sources for intermediate and capital goods as well. The Republic of China on Taiwan, in effect, has embarked upon a program of secondary import substitution to reduce its dependency on Japan for the provision of such goods. One result is that the increased mechanization of Taiwanese agriculture will be accomplished largely through Taiwanese production. As we have seen, one of Taiwan's heaviest foreign exchange burdens has been the trade deficit with Japan that has resulted from the import of transportation equipment, chemicals, electrical machinery, and farm equipment. In 1972 Japan supplied 53, 60, 75, and 64 percent of Taiwan's total imports of these products. With the development of machine and producer-goods industries, Taiwanese planners anticipate a reduction in the trade deficit with Japan. Taiwan already is producing many of the intermediate and producer goods it has hitherto imported.

Part of the current program of secondary import substitution has been a concerted effort to deepen industry by backward and forward linkages. One of the "Ten Major Projects" that was contained in the six-year plan of 1976-1981 was the establishment of an integrated steel plant with a projected production sufficient to meet domestic need. In accordance with the overall policy, and specifically to stabilize the price of steel products in the face of

---

13. Ibid., December 10, 1979, p. 2.
14. Ranis, "Industrial Development," p. 258.

rising steel costs, phase one of the China Steel Corporation development was completed at the end of 1977.[15] In 1979 crude steel production in Taiwan reached 4.3 million metric tons, an increase of almost a million tons over the 3.4 million tons produced in 1978—a 26.1 percent increment. Today, three developing economies—the Republic of China on Taiwan, the Republic of South Korea, and Brazil—lead the developing nations in the production of crude steel.[16] By 1982 annual production on Taiwan is expected to reach 8 million metric tons, and by 1988 production will exceed 13 million metric tons.[17] The Republic of China expects to export 1.1 million metric tons of steel products in 1980 and to supplement the Kaohsiung steel complex by building in central Taiwan a mill with an annual capacity of 8 million tons.[18] In 1979 the China Steel Corporation (CSC) became the principal foreign supplier of steel products to Japan.[19] Recently the American Society of Mechanical Engineers certified the CSC as a qualified material manufacturer of nuclear quality steel. The CSC is the fifteenth company in the world to receive such certification.[20]

A major consumer of the pig iron, billets, plate, wire rods, and bar-in-coil steel products of the CSC is the China Shipbuilding Corporation (CSBC), which until 1957 built only fishing vessels ranging from 75 to 500 tons displacement. Two decades later, in June 1977, the CSBC launched the 445,000 ton supertanker *Burmah Endeavor,* the third largest ship afloat. At present, Taiwanese shipbuilding firms construct 70 percent of all components on ships fabricated on the island; full component construction is limited only by a shortage of workers skilled in metallurgy and in the use of precision instruments. The shipyards of Kaohsiung and Keelung are now among the twelve leading shipbuilding complexes in the world.[21] During the next decade the Ministry of Communications has contracted for the construction of 99 containerized cargo carriers, crude carriers, and bulk carriers. The building program is expected to increase the Republic of China's fleet of flag-carriers so that by 1989 70 percent of inbound bulk commodities and 40 percent of inbound and outbound general cargoes will be carried by national-flag vessels, thus giving the island greater control over its lifelines. The ships, among which will be six 125,000 ton bulk carriers of coke and iron ore for the CSC, will be built by the CSBC, utilizing the growing production of the CSC.

15. See Bank of America, *China Steel Corporation: US $80,000,000 Term Loan* (San Francisco: Bank of America, February 1979), Information Memorandum.
16. *China Post,* January 31, 1980, p. 4.
17. Ibid., February 29, 1980, p. 4.
18. Ibid., March 8, 1980, p. 3.
19. Ibid., August 30, 1979, p. 4.
20. Ibid., March 11, 1980, p. 4.
21. Ibid., March 4, 1980, p. 4.

The Republic of China's aircraft industry has similarly expanded in the course of the same program. The Aero Industry Development Center (AIDC) at Taichung, utilizing the Avco Lycoming T53 turboshaft and turboprop engines, can now produce a modified version of the North American T-28 trainer. The center also coproduces a sophisticated fighter aircraft, the Northrop F-5E, indigenously supplying about 33 percent of its components and 60 percent of the wiring harness, restricted once again by the shortage of workers with the metallurgical, electronic, and technical skills required in the tooling of high-thrust, high-performance jet engines.[22] Nonetheless, the center has undertaken to design and produce two original aircraft, one a light, twin-turboprop military transport, designated XC-2 and powered by two 1400 horsepower Avco Lycoming T53-L-701 engines, and the other a twin-engined military trainer powered by two turbojets. While neither design is sophisticated, involving little that is aerodynamically or structurally advanced, both represent advances in the capability of the Republic of China's aircraft industry since the center was established in 1969 and further reduce dependence on foreign suppliers. The center now includes an aeronautical research and development laboratory, an aircraft manufacturing facility, and an engine plant. The completion in 1978 of a wind tunnel that generates air flows up to Mach 0.3 will increase the research and development capability of the AIDC considerably.[23]

Automobile construction on Taiwan involves six manufacturing companies which produce more than 100,000 complete units annually under a technical cooperation agreement with foreign automotive manufacturers. More than 300 auto-parts companies provide springs, tires, car windowpanes, and electrical supplies both for indigenous production and for export. By 1976 the Taiwanese rubber industry annually produced more than a million automobile tires and 9.5 million sets of motorcycle tires and tubes.[24] In January 1980 the production of automobile tires was up 33 percent over that of the preceding year.[25]

In yet another instance of backward linkage and secondary import substitution, the petrochemical industry of Taiwan now produces enough of some major petrochemical raw materials to meet the needs of the domestic textile and chemical industries. The production of ethylene glycol and acrylonitrile, the bases for the production of man-made fiber filament, now

22. Donald E. Fink, "Nationalists Update Fighter Force," *Aviation Week and Space Technology* 108, no. 22 (May 29, 1978): 14-16.
23. Fink, "Center Designs Two Aircraft," ibid., 108, no. 23 (June 5, 1978): 14-16.
24. Han Lih-wu, *Taiwan Today* (Taipei: Cheng Chung Publisher, 1977), p. 137.
25. *China Post,* March 4, 1980, p. 4.

exceeds domestic Taiwanese demand. Taiwan's production of propylene glycol and polypropylene glycol similarly exceeds the domestic demand of the chemical industry.

The expanded production of more sophisticated machine products has not only allowed for import substitution but has also permitted Taiwan to expand its exports of intermediate and capital goods throughout Southeast Asia. In keeping with the notion of comparative advantage, Taiwan continues to export relatively cheap, high-quality, labor-intensive products to the developed countries (DCs), while selling more capital-intensive intermediate and producer goods to its neighboring LDC trading partners. Given the advantage of lower transport costs compared to potential DC competitors and the greater availability of technically competent labor compared to any other LDC producer, Taiwan has become a supplier of producer and capital goods to the developing economies of Southeast Asia. Thus, in 1977 Taiwan exported 79 complete plants valued at $22.5 million to its various LDC neighbors. In 1978 117 fully equipped plants, valued at $28.11 million, were exported. In 1979 the value of whole plant sales to be exported was estimated to be more than double that of 1978. A single synthetic fiber plant worth $23 million was scheduled for construction in Indonesia in 1979, to be supplemented throughout the Southeast Asia region by whole plant transfers for paper production, plastic processing, and cement, textile, and rolled steel manufacturing. Since 1978 Taiwan has undertaken whole plant transfers to Africa, the Middle East, and Latin America.[26]

The export of machinery and intermediate goods has accelerated under the current program. In 1976 machinery worth $347 million was exported; in 1979 machinery exported was valued at $600 million. In 1977 Taiwanese technicians accompanied machinery exports to the Middle East to complete an electrification project and to operate and maintain a power plant and transmission system in Al-Baha, Saudi Arabia.

Thus, by the beginning of the 1980s the Republic of China on Taiwan had begun seriously to address the problems of declining agricultural productivity, an increasing shortage of unskilled and semiskilled labor, and the economy's dependence on imported producer materials and intermediate capital goods. The program to stabilize agriculture has begun, and the industrial sector has undertaken a shift into technology- and capital-intensive production with all its labor-saving and increasingly high-wage implications. Backward and forward linkages in industry are reducing dependence on the import of intermediate and producer goods whose accelerating costs threaten Taiwan's favorable balance of payments. With these developments the

26. Ibid., September 25, 1979, p. 4; October 26, 1979, p. 4; and January 3, 1980, p. 4.

economy of Taiwan has deepened and matured. What remains less tractable are fuel costs (primarily imported oil, which currently supplies about 70 percent of the island's needs), a world-wide rate of inflation that threatens every nation, and the insecurities that attend world trade.

In the effort to offset dependency on oil imports, the Republic of China has begun the construction of three nuclear power generating facilities, the first of which began production in December 1978. By 1985 the three plants are expected to produce about 5 million kilowatts. Plans anticipate between ten and twenty such plants in operation by the turn of the century, capable of generating from 25 to 50 million kilowatts. At the same time three new (probably) coal-fired, thermal, power-generating plants are being constructed at Hsiehho, Hsingta, and Chungpu. By 1989 Taiwan expects to reduce its dependence on imported fuel oil for power generation to about 36.5 percent. To assure current fuel oil supplies the government has entered into special relations with Saudi Arabia, which supplies 40 percent of the island's petroleum. An upgrading of relations with South Africa has assured Taiwan of a continuous supply of atomic fuel for its nuclear reactors. Nonetheless, the costs of energy supply will continue to increase, given world energy supply conditions. The increasing cost of fuel has caused inevitable inflationary pressures in Taiwan that the government originally hoped to hold to a 6 percent annual increase.

Restraining inflationary pressures to that level would have constituted something of an economic miracle. Wholesale prices and urban consumer prices increased 13.84 and 9.75 percent respectively in 1979. The prices of imported goods rose 16.34 percent during the same period. These pressures translated themselves into a 3.84 percent increase in consumer prices during the first month of 1980—an annual inflation rate of 46 percent.[27] These increases were fueled in part by the announcement by the Chinese Petroleum Corporation in December 1979 that prices of more than a dozen oil products would increase between 31.7 and 74.07 percent.[28] By the beginning of 1980 the Council for Economic Planning and Development readjusted its projections concerning the anticipated rate of inflation from the original 6 percent to an estimated, but still unrealistic, 7.5 percent.[29] The cost of imported oil increased from $2.2 billion in 1979 to $4.4 billion in 1980.[30]

The Republic of China thus is faced with many of the same problems that beset other relatively open market economies in the contemporary

27. Ibid., January 11, 1980, p. 4; January 26, 1980, p. 3; and March 4, 1980, p. 4.
28. Ibid., December 28, 1979, p. 4.
29. Ibid., January 3, 1980, p. 4. In the first eight months of 1980 consumer prices rose 17.62 percent over the same period in 1979. Ibid., November 7, 1980, p. 2.
30. Ibid., January 23, 1980, p. 4.

world. To reduce their heavy dependence on imports, the prices of which depend on conditions of trade that Taiwan can neither control nor significantly influence, businessmen are attempting to augment supplies and acquire access to raw materials and markets through foreign investment. Like the Japanese who preceded them, Taiwanese entrepreneurs have begun to establish undertakings in foreign markets, utilizing their comparative advantage in technical expertise and marketing. Taiwanese business has begun to invest in manufacturing facilities and marketing outlets in foreign countries—in textiles, petrochemicals, and the production of construction materials. In addition, there has been some investment in overseas resource and raw materials supply. Taiwanese investors have begun to invest in timberland in Indonesia, corn-growing farms in Thailand, uranium exploration in Paraguay, and oil refineries in Hawaii.[31] All these investments will provide the Republic of China with foreign earnings that will be recycled to promote export sales and augment foreign exchange. Eventually, such investments and acquisitions will offer Taiwanese producers and consumers greater assurance of continuity of supply and access to raw materials and markets at potentially more advantageous terms than would be the case without external investment.[32]

Taiwanese foreign investment has grown steadily, particularly since 1975. Between 1959 and 1979 there were 91 foreign investments, amounting to $26.5 million, undertaken by investors from the Republic of China, while in 1977 such investments totaled almost $14 million. In 1979 applications for more than $25 million in foreign investments were approved by the Ministry of Economic Affairs.[33] Such figures probably significantly understate the amount of foreign investments, since many investments are made directly by Taiwanese entrepreneurs without clearance with the ministry. Actual foreign investments are probably fourteen to fifteen times the value of approved investments and have been undertaken by Taiwanese investors directly or in joint ventures in Southeast Asian countries without the intervention of the Ministry of Economic Affairs. Since 1975 an increasing proportion of the foreign investment has been going into resource and fuel augmentation and uranium exploration; an undisclosed sum was invested in a joint venture in oil refining in Hawaii. Taiwanese capital is involved in a similar $800 million joint venture in Indonesia.[34]

---

31. Ibid., January 19, 1980 p. 3; January 23, 1980, p. 4.
32. Yuan-li Wu and Kung-chia Yeh, "Taiwan's External Economic Relations," in *Growth, Distribution and Social Change: Essays on the Economy of the Republic of China,* ed. Yuan-li Wu and Kung-chia Yeh (Baltimore: University of Maryland School of Law, 1978), pp. 197-198.
33. *China Post,* October 17, 1979, p. 4; and January 29, 1980, p. 4.
34. Ibid., March 7, 1980, p. 4.

While all these sums are relatively small, they signal that the historically common occurrence of a developing country itself maturing into an investor country is being repeated in the case of the Republic of China. At present, most of the investments are in manufacturing industries, construction and construction materials, and textiles; but increasing sums are being committed to the development of mineral fuel and agricultural raw materials. Assured access to raw materials, along with heavy industries capable of providing industrial raw materials for processing industries, constitutes a mature productive system maximally insulated from destabilization and disruption. As the industries of Taiwan are deepened, the productive process moves further "upstream." The steel industry produces industrial raw materials for shipbuilding, construction, and automotive enterprises. The petrochemical industry now locally produces many of the chemical raw materials necessary for the man-made fiber processing industry. Since basic raw materials vary in price more than midstream processed goods,[35] and since such goods can be obtained, in principle, from more suppliers, Taiwan purchasers should have greater access to supplies and purchasing advantages with the development of the more mature system.

While all this has been transpiring, Taiwan has continued to maintain a high level of foreign trade. In 1979 the value of trade increased 30 percent to a total of $30.9 billion. Taiwan's bilateral trade with the United States reached $9 billion, making the Republic of China America's seventh largest trading partner. In 1980 the Republic of China increased its foreign trade 26.6 percent over that of 1979, to a level of $39 billion, while it maintained the present favorable balance of trade.[36] The Republic of China has now become the leading exporter of sewing machines in the world, and it is second only to Japan in the export of man-made fibers.[37] Textile exports, in fact, remain the largest foreign exchange earner for Taiwan with total exports in 1980 exceeding $4.3 billion, representing more than 20 percent of total exports. The United States remains the single largest market for Taiwanese exports, purchasing 35.1 percent of the total.[38] As a supplier of goods for the United States, the Republic of China is exceeded only by two of the nine European Economic Community members—West Germany and Great Britain.[39] As a market for American goods, Taiwan is half as valuable as France and Italy combined. It purchases ten times more American goods than does mainland China.

---

35. See Wei Wou, *Sino-Korean Trade Competition: An Econometric Analysis* (Taipei: Asia and the World Forum, 1977), pp. 4-5.
36. *China Post,* February 5, 1981, p. 1; and February 25, 1981, p. 2.
37. Ibid., February 5, 1981, p. 4.
38. Ibid., January 21, 1981, p. 2.
39. Wu and Yeh, "Taiwan's External Economic Relations," pp. 211-212.

While the United States will remain the Republic of China's major trading partner for the foreseeable future, Taiwan has begun to diversify its foreign trade to reduce the degree of trading partner concentration that has characterized its economic history. In 1979 trade with Europe was expanded. Trade with West Germany exceeded $1.4 billion, and that with Great Britain exceeded $700 million. European trade now totals 13 percent of Taiwan's entire foreign trade.

To foster diversification in trading partners, the government on Taiwan has removed restrictions on trade with Eastern Europe (with the exception of the Soviet Union), and Taiwanese industrialists have participated in trade fairs in Poland, Hungary, Rumania, East Germany, and Czechoslovakia. Excluding trade conducted through third-party countries, Taiwanese exports to Eastern Europe during the first year of trade reached $22 million. Trade missions have been dispatched to Latin America, where there is a potential market for machinery, electrical appliances, electronic and plastics products, and processed foods. Trade with Saudi Arabia now exceeds $1.3 billion. Substantial trade is now being conducted with Hong Kong, Singapore, Kuwait, Canada, Australia, and the nations of Southeast Asia. With the upgrading of diplomatic relations with the Republic of South Africa, the Republic of China expects to expand its trade and commercial relations in southern Africa. Because of prevailing international economic conditions, with the increasing pressure for protection for home markets in those countries beset by economic dislocation, diversification of trading partners has become a necessity for Taiwan's continued economic well-being.

Irrespective of inflation and the prevailing energy crisis, economic growth in the Republic of China (in real terms) was 8.0 percent (with manufacturing growing at about 25 percent) for 1979, considerably above the world average of 3.4 percent; this rate earned Taiwan a place among the countries with the highest rates of growth. For the same period, the GNP growth in the United States was less than 2 percent, the average for Europe was 2.5 percent, and the economic growth of Japan was 4.5 percent.

In 1979 the Republic of China was one of the few countries in Asia that registered a trade surplus. The Republic of South Korea, Taiwan's principal trade competitor, registered a net loss in foreign exchange while the Republic of China realized a trade surplus of about $1 billion. In 1979 Taiwan's exports grew at about twice the rate of South Korea's.[40] Taiwanese exports of textiles, manufactured goods, heavy and intermediate industrial machinery and machine parts, electronic commodities, electrical appliances,

---

40. *China Post,* November 19, 1979, p. 2; January 3, 1980, p. 4; January 21, 1980, p. 2; and February 25, 1980, p. 2.

steel and petrochemical products, and processed foods are all expected to be competitive in the international markets of the 1980s.

Under a plan for the 1980s recently proposed by the Council for Economic Planning and Development, the economy of Taiwan is expected to achieve substantial maturity by the end of the decade. The average rate of domestic economic growth is expected to be about 8 percent annually with the growth of the GNP anticipated at 7.8 percent. By 1989 the GNP of the Republic of China is expected to be $70.2 billion, with the per capita GNP expected to be $6,107 (compared to the current $2,140). At the end of the decade industrial production will account for 57.1 percent of the net domestic product with agriculture constituting 6 percent and the service industry 36.9 percent.[41] The structural transformation of a basically agricultural economy into a modern and industrialized economic system will be essentially completed. Should the Republic of China on Taiwan achieve its goals, it will have undergone a transformation unique in the twentieth century. In less than four decades Taiwan will have achieved a level of maturation that took other developing nations far longer to attain. Taiwanese industry, as measured by industry's share in the nation's net domestic product, will have expanded by 40 percentage points in four decades. By comparison, industry's share of Britain's net domestic product rose by only 11 percentage points during 40 years (1801-1841) of that nation's economic development; and during Japan's development from 1882 to 1927, industry's share increased by about 22 percentage points.[42] Moreover, if current policies are pursued, economic development will have been accomplished with rising, and surprisingly equalitarian, rates of growth both in per capita income and consumption. The average rate of growth in per capita consumption was approximately 3.0 percent per annum from 1951 through 1962, accelerating to 5.4 percent from 1962 through 1974. This was interrupted by the oil crises of 1972-1974, only to resume its upward growth thereafter. Between 1952 and 1973, per capita consumption increased by 250 percent. The fact that Japan only doubled its per capita consumption in the forty years between 1924 and 1964 indicates how significant this increase was.[43]

All of this has been accomplished with a remarkable degree of family income equity among the citizens of the Republic of China.[44] Sun Yat-sen

---

41. Ibid., January 25, 1980, p. 1; and March 7, 1980, p. 1.
42. Kung-chia Yeh, "Economic Growth: An Overview," in *Growth, Distribution and Social Change,* pp. 25-26.
43. See Simon Kuznets, "Trends in Level and Structure of Consumption," in *Economic Growth,* ed. L. Klein and K. Ohkawa (Homewood, Ill.: Irwin Publishers, 1968), p. 198.
44. See John C. H. Fei, Gustav Ranis, and Shirley W. Y. Kuo, *Growth with Equity: The Taiwan Case* (New York: Oxford, 1979).

had made such equity a critical component of his plans for the development of China—and it is evident that considerations of economic justice influenced the programs implemented on Taiwan. However inadequate some of the statistical data may be—and there is no reason to believe that the most relevant data from Taiwan is any less credible than data obtained anywhere in the developing world—all the evidence available supports the contention that income distribution on Taiwan has been increasingly equalitarian. Although the information collected during the early years of Taiwan's development derives from small samples drawn from matched rather than randomly obtained probability samples, those data obtained after 1962 are as hard as any available.[45] That data indicates that economic development on Taiwan benefited *all* income groups and that from 1950 to the present the economic position of the poor has improved not only absolutely, but relatively as well. Whatever underreporting there may be by higher income groups in the effort to escape taxation, there clearly was a dramatic shift in income distribution on Taiwan in the direction of greater equality during the process of economic development. Between 1960 and the present the income of the lowest income groups has increased almost twice as fast as the growth of the economy as a whole.[46] Thus, even if the data from the early period are dismissed as suspect, the evidence from the 1960s indicates a high degree of overall income equality on Taiwan.

During the 1960s the 40 percent of the population on Taiwan with the lowest income received about 20 percent of the nation's income. By comparison, the average income share of the lowest 40 percent of the population in all LDCs was 12.5 percent, and in half of all LDCs the income share of the lowest two quintiles of the population was only 9 percent. The United Nations has identified those countries in which the lowest 40 percent of the population received more than 17 percent of total income as "low inequality" economic systems.[47] The income distribution pattern on Taiwan would

---

45. See the criticisms of Hill Gates, "Dependence and the Part-time Proletariat in Taiwan," *Modern China* 5, no. 3 (July 1979): 384.

46. Samuel P. S. Ho, *Economic Development of Taiwan* (New Haven: Yale University Press, 1978), pp. 140-141; Republic of China, Council for Economic Planning and Development, *Social Welfare Indicators, Republic of China* (Taipei: Council for Economic Planning and Development, September 1979), p. 9, Table I-3; Chien Ting-an, "Economic Growth, Income Distribution, and Fiscal Policy," *China Forum* 5, no. 1 (January 1978): 1-36; Republic of China, Auditing Department of the Executive Yuan, *Investigation and Statistical Report on Individual Income Distribution in the Taiwan Area* (Taipei: Auditing Department of the Executive Yuan, 1977).

47. Montek Ahluwalia, "Income Inequality: Some Dimensions of the Problem," in *Redistribution with Growth,* ed. Hollis Chenery et al. (Oxford: Oxford University Press, 1974), pp. 8-9; see Irma Adelman and Cynthia T. Morris, *Economic Growth and Social Inequality in Developing Countries* (Stanford: Stanford University Press, 1973).

thus qualify its economic system as one of low inequality. In fact, the present pattern of income distribution on Taiwan is remarkably similar to that of Japan and the United States. The income distribution in the Republic of China in the 1960s and the 1970s was among the most equal in the world, comparable not only to that of the United States, Japan, and the United Kingdom, but to such socialist countries as Yugoslavia and Poland as well. There is every indication that it is more egalitarian than that of Communist China.[48]

One of the major achievements of development on Taiwan has been the ability to combine high rates of savings with increases in per capita consumption and a surprising degree of equity in the distribution of income. Some nations—like Pakistan—have achieved relatively rapid growth, but at the expense of equity. Others—like Sri Lanka—have provided equity, but at the expense of economic and industrial growth. Taiwan, on the other hand, has provided for a more equitable distribution of incomes than Sri Lanka while maintaining a high rate of growth.[49] For a country that has enjoyed such rapid growth—a phenomenon generally associated with increasing disparities of income—Taiwan's income "is exceptionally equally distributed." World Bank data makes the Republic of China on Taiwan the developing country with the most equitable distribution of income.[50] That equity has been accomplished largely through the implementation of the programs embodied in the works of Sun Yat-sen: initial asset redistribution through rent reduction and land redistribution which significantly altered future income streams, subsequently sustained by the relatively uniform dispersal of industry throughout the island which allowed nonagricultural wage supplements to farm families. At the same time nonincome benefits were widely distributed, making Taiwan's family income equity possible in circumstances of rapid growth—rendering the island's economic history singular, if not unique, among the late developers of the second half of the twentieth century.[51]

---

48. Ahluwalia, "Income Inequality," Table I.1; and Yuan-li Wu, *Income Distribution in the Process of Economic Growth of the Republic of China* (Baltimore: University of Maryland School of Law, 1977), pp. 7-8, 32-42; see Jan S. Prybyla, *The Societal Objective of Wealth, Growth, Stability and Equity in Taiwan* (Baltimore: University of Maryland School of Law, 1978), pp. 28-31.

49. Keith Griffin, "An Assessment of Development in Taiwan," *World Development* 1, no. 6 (June 1973): 40.

50. Ian M. D. Little, "An Economic Reconnaissance," in *Economic Growth and Structural Change in Taiwan,* ed. Walter Galenson (Ithaca, N.Y.: Cornell University Press, 1979), p. 498; Kuo Wan-yong, *The Past and the Prospects of the Income Distribution in Taiwan* (Taipei: Institute of Economics, August 1976).

51. Kuo Wan-yong, "The Goal of 'Equality and Affluence' and Government Policies," *China Forum* 3, no. 2 (July 1976): 85-94; Gustav Ranis, "Taiwan," in *Redistribution with Growth,* pp. 285-290; Simon Kuznets, "Economic Growth and Income

Among the nonincome benefits that have become increasingly available to all on Taiwan is education. The level of education in the Republic of China is about four times the norm for a country with its level of per capita GNP. In 1946, upon retrocession of Taiwan to the control of the Republic of China, there were only 4 colleges, 215 middle schools, and 1,130 elementary schools on the island. By 1972 there were 81 universities and colleges, 842 middle schools, and 2,193 primary schools in service. By that time more than 12.5 percent of college age groups, 57.9 percent of middle-school cohorts, and 98.13 percent of primary-school age groups were attending educational institutions at their respective levels.[52] In 1950 there were on the average 4.2 schools per 100 square kilometers on Taiwan; by 1979 there were 13.3 per 100 square kilometers, an increase of about 320 percent. In 1950 there were 139.6 students per 1,000 persons in the population; in 1979 there were 262.3 per 1,000. During the same period the student-teacher ratio declined from 36:1 to 28:1 and the average class size from 52 students per class to 46. In 1950 80 percent of the children in the age group between 6 and 12 regularly attended school; in 1979 more than 99 percent were attending school. In 1950 there were 62 high schools with a total of 18,866 students; in 1979 there were 187 schools with a student population of 177,647. In 1950 there were 77 vocational schools with 34,436 students, and in 1979 there were 184 such schools with 312,061 students—an increase in students in excess of 800 percent. At the time of the retrocession of Taiwan to the Republic of China there very few, if any, students in institutions of higher learning. By 1950 there were 6,665 students in seven institutions of higher learning: one university, three colleges, and three junior colleges. By 1979 317,188 students attended 101 institutions of advanced learning and 185 affiliated research facilities. In fewer than thirty years the number of students undertaking advanced studies increased 4,659 percent.[53]

Access to education beyond the first six years of schooling (ages 6 through 12) is via public examination. Schooling through grade nine is free of placement testing; but after graduation from junior middle school, students undertake a series of tests that constitute quality-control filters into senior middle school, senior vocational school, or a five-year junior college program. After graduation from senior middle school, students can apply for the Joint College Entrance Examination (JCEE) for admission to a four-year program leading to a bachelor's degree. The JCEE is composed of nine subtests: Chinese, English, mathematics, Sun's Three Principles of the People,

Inequality," *American Economic Review* 45, no. 1 (March 1955): 1-28.

52. Wei Yung, "Modernization Process in Taiwan: An Allocative Analysis," *Asian Survey* 16, no. 3 (March 1976): 262-263.

53. Republic of China, Ministry of Education, *Educational Statistics of the Republic of China* (Taipei: Ministry of Education, 1979), pp. 14-16.

history, geography, biology, chemistry, and physics. Whatever criticisms have been leveled against the testing process, the machine grading of these examinations produces unbiased results, favoring neither rich nor poor. Once admitted to college or university, almost all candidates successfully complete their programs (the failure rate is less than 7 percent). With the increasing equality of income distribution, cost restraints are less and less likely to keep students with low incomes from attending institutions of higher learning. Because of increasing government investment in education, tuition costs have remained relatively low. That more and more farm children are attending not only primary school but middle school and college as well suggests the increasing equality of access to education. As the population engaged in agricultural activities in Taiwan increased by 128 percent between 1948 and 1971, the number of farm children attending primary schools increased by 257 percent; those attending middle school increased by 2,826 percent; and those pursuing a college degree increased by 16,820 percent.

Although wealth and status seem to convey privilege on Taiwan (as they seem to everywhere) with the wealthy and those of mainland Chinese origin having greater access to the best educational establishments, it seems equally evident that education has become increasingly available to all.[54] By 1976 more than a quarter of the entire population of Taiwan was attending school, with proportionately more students pursuing advanced education there than was the case in Great Britain, Italy, or West Germany.[55]

The increasing levels of consumption and the comparative equity of its distribution have been supplemented not only by educational benefits but by improvements in almost every dimension of social welfare. In 1950, for example, the life expectancy of males on Taiwan was 52.9 and that of females was 56.3. In 1976 the life expectancy of males was 68.8 and that of females was 73.7.[56]

Infant mortality declined from 3.7 percent to 1.6 percent of all full-term pregnancies during the same period. Infant deaths (under one year of age) per 1,000 live births declined from 33.7 in 1953 to 17.5 in 1970. In 1954 there was one hospital bed available for every 2,988 persons on Taiwan. In 1978 there was one bed per 457 persons. The number of medical care

54. *China Times,* June 27, 1976, p. 1.
55. Jan S. Prybyla, "Economic Development in Taiwan," in *China and the Taiwan Issue,* ed. Hungdah Chiu (New York: Praeger, 1979), p. 120; Wei, "Modernization Process in Taiwan," p. 263; Martin M. C. Yang, *Socio-Economic Results of Land Reform in Taiwan* (Honolulu: East-West Center Press, 1970), pp. 367-383.
56. Republic of China, Directorate-General of Budget, Accounting and Statistics, *Statistical Yearbook of the Republic of China* (Taipei: Directorate-General of Budget, Accounting and Statistics, 1977), pp. 44-45, Table 18.

facilities increased from the 1,000 in service in 1954 to the 9,919 operative in 1978. Although the number of physicians has increased during the same period from 5,523 to 12,509, the rapid growth of the population has allowed the ratio of physicians to potential patients to decline only from 1:1,556 to 1:1,357.[57] Twenty-seven provincial, 9 city and county, and 9 municipal hospitals constitute the nucleus of the public health service, supplemented by 347 health stations at township and village levels throughout Taiwan. These are augmented by 9,527 private hospitals and clinics, among which are missionary and charitable establishments. Government Employees' Health Insurance and Labor Health Insurance, covering about 13.5 percent of the total population, provide services to beneficiaries. Schools maintain a nurse in service for first aid and routine physical examinations and immunizations, as well as health and hygiene instruction.

The little comparative data for housing on Taiwan indicates that Taiwan's housing standards are relatively good compared to those of other developing countries for which data are available. In 1975 the government initiated a housing program for workers; but given the apparent backlog of demand, the program will have to be more vigorously pursued if all housing needs are to be met soon. Progress, as we have seen, has been made in terms of residence electrification (with 88 percent of rural dwellings provided with electrical power as early as 1970), water supply, and sanitation facilities. But only a relatively small proportion of the national product has been committed to housing, and at present the average dwelling contains only about one hundred square feet of living space per capita.

The government has made efforts to provide the rudiments of social insurance and increased public services. The major social insurance program now in effect on Taiwan is the Labor Health Insurance scheme covering all industrial establishments and commercial firms with more than ten employees. In June 1978 more than 2.01 million (out of about 6.5 million) workers were insured under the program, which provides maternity benefits and injury insurance (70 percent of the wage for up to six months and 50 percent for the next six months) for job-related injuries. If an injury is not job-related, compensation of 50 percent of wage for six months is provided. A lump-sum payment, equivalent to up to forty-five months of wages, is provided upon retirement at sixty years of age. Death payments on the insured are provided the immediate family. The most important provision of the program is that which affords medical and hospital services to insured individuals. Under the program, medical care and drugs are free, as is the first month of hospitalization. After that period the insured is billed for half the

57. Republic of China, National Health Administration, *Health Statistics: Republic of China* (Taipei: National Health Administration, 1978), p. 23, Table 8.

cost of meals. There are no public or private old-age pension schemes in Taiwan, with aged workers falling back on savings or on the traditional extended family for support. There is no effective system of unemployment compensation.

At present a number of programs are being drafted to improve the social insurance and welfare benefits system of the Republic of China. As it exists, however, the system "is by no means a negligible achievement for a country that has so recently emerged from an Asian standard of living."[58] But with the reconstitution of the Chinese Federation of Labor in 1976, the social insurance system will probably have to respond to the pressures exerted by organized labor—and expand and enhance available benefits. About 30 percent of the employees in industrial enterprises were unionized by 1976; and although union activities in Taiwan have been anything but aggressive in the past, it is predictable that as the economy further matures, economic as well as political considerations will provide that unions take part in making the decisions that influence the allocation of benefits throughout the system.

Taiwanese workers receive respectable wages by Asian standards, but it is doubtful if Asian living standards constitute their immediate reference. Their Japanese, not to speak of their American, counterparts earn many times more than do Taiwanese workers, and the discrepancy between male and female wages is still scandalous. While it may be true that Taiwanese women still anticipate a more traditional family role as their objective in life, there is every reason to believe that with the growing labor shortage they will address themselves to more equitable income distribution. While women in Taiwan currently see their employment as temporary, they do constitute about 33 percent of the labor force in manufacturing. Because unmarried women live at home (or in factory dormitories), their earnings are not expected, at present, to provide for fully independent maintenance.[59] As the Republic of China on Taiwan attains greater economic maturity, such inequities will have to be resolved if for no other reason than to insulate male workers (at their own insistence) from the competition of lower-paid female labor.

Finally, by the mid-1970s the government on Taiwan had begun to address itself to the problem of the hard-core poor—those who are unable to work and who are bereft of all assets and income. As a beginning, the

58. Walter Galenson, "The Labor Force, Wages, and Living Standards," in *Economic Growth and Structural Change in Taiwan,* p. 445.
59. Norma Diamond, "Women and Industry in Taiwan," *Modern China* 5, no. 3 (July 1979): 317-339; see Galenson, "The Labor Force, Wages, and Living Standards," p. 418.

authorities have established a minimum subsistence level of about $100 per annum per household below which institutional and relief care will be provided. Active job placement is provided the poor, and occupational training opportunities are afforded. Part of the current "antipoverty" program involves encouraging the children of poor families to attend school. Further, to extend the antipoverty program beyond the level of government effort alone, the government sponsors community production, marketing, and welfare activities. Emergency relief and long-term loans have been made available in the effort to minimize the emergence of new "poverty households," with long-term aid for those who simply cannot provide for themselves. Because the subsistence level is set so low, less than 1 percent of the total number of households on Taiwan fall below the requisite poverty line that makes them eligible for government assistance. In 1975 that number involved only 25,700 households out of a total of 2.9 million.

Nonetheless, the first steps toward a modern welfare system have been taken. Presently wages, which remain low by the standards of contemporary developed economies, are supplemented by employer-supplied fringe benefits that include food, transportation, dormitory facilities, and clothing allowances. With the prevailing low unemployment rate, the reconstitution of labor unions, increased sophistication of the electorate, and the expectations aroused by steady improvement in living conditions and consumption, it is predictable that in the reasonably near future social and welfare insurance programs will expand and deepen, wages will improve, and the general standard of living will be enhanced by a variety of private and public supplements. That equity will continue to govern the expected increase in wages in the future as it has in the past will constitute testimony of the Kuomintang's commitment to the social goals of Sun.[60]

---

60. See Wei Eh, *Chieh-k'ai Tai-wan ching-chi fa-chan chih mi* [Revealing the mystery of Taiwan's economic development], (Taipei: Yuan Ching Publishing Company, 1980); Chang Ch'i-yün, *San-min chu-i mo-fan-sheng chih chien-she* [The construction of a San-min chu-i model province], (Taipei: Chinese Cultural Committee 1956).

V

Taiwan as a Model of Development

> By 1990 Taiwan will have completed a transition . . . placing it among developed countries. This quantum jump would, were it not for a closed-mind ideological bias, serve as a model for others in the Third World and LDC camps.[1]

Perhaps because Taiwan's economic performance has been so unusual, there has been a tendency to treat its experience as a "special case" having little that might be instructive to less developed communities.[2] It would be idle, Alice Amsden has argued, "to hold Taiwan up as an example of capitalist development for other poor countries to follow."[3] Why this should be so is not immediately evident.

Like most LDCs the Republic of China on Taiwan is both small in size and lacking in natural resources. It has a relatively small total population but a high demographic density. Its citizenry numbers about 17 million with a population density of 476 persons per square kilometer—one of the highest densities in the world. Its 13,900 square miles are spread over an island about 240 miles long and about 90 miles at its greatest width. About the size of Massachusetts and Connecticut combined, it possesses very little subsoil resources—no minerals or fossil fuels to speak of. It is more like the remaining LDCs than like any of the socialist or capitalist major powers. It has neither the continental dimensions, population, resources, nor markets of scale possessed by mainland China, the Soviet Union, or the United States. Like most of the LDCs, Taiwan has had a recent history of colonial dependency. At the time it commenced development a largely monocultural, agrarian, productive system was in place, with a high degree of trading partner concentration. At the outset of its economic development, Taiwan,

---

1. Julian Weiss, *Taiwan: One Year After United States-China Normalization* (Washington, D.C.: Government Printing Office, 1980, p. 86.
2. Norma Diamond, "Introduction," *Modern China* 5, No. 3 (July 1979): 280.
3. Alice H. Amsden, "Taiwan's Economic History," *Modern China* 5, no. 3 (July 1979): 373.

like most LDCs, was characterized by a dearth of indigenous capital. Given the features it shares with other LDCs, it is not evident why Taiwan should constitute a "special," rather than a "model," instance of development.

Unlike most LDCs, of course, Taiwan is an island. But there is no self-evident reason why this fact should render its developmental experience unique. Some island economies, like England's and Japan's, have been "less developed" at some point, and others remain largely so (e.g., Sri Lanka, the Philippines, and Indonesia). There is little to suggest that island economies either prosper or fail to prosper because of their geographic circumstances. The further fact that unlike most LDCs Taiwan shoulders a heavy defense burden which consumes about 9 percent of its total GNP could hardly provide the advantage that would make its economic experience atypical.[4] If anything, the maintenance of an expensive military establishment would constitute a constraint on economic development and make Taiwan's experience special only in the sense of being more remarkable.

Several factors are frequently cited as special advantages that distinguish Taiwan's experience sufficiently from those of other LDCs to reduce its candidacy as a model of development. The Japanese provision of primary education for the population of Taiwan during their occupation of the island, for example, is often cited as a special advantage enjoyed at the commencement of development. As a matter of fact, at the time of Taiwan's retrocession to the Republic of china, 55 percent of its total population was reckoned illiterate. By 1952 when Taiwan commenced its development, the illiteracy rate for those over six years of age had been reduced to 42.1 percent.[5] If one compares these statistics with those of contemporary LDCs, one finds that the average illiteracy rate of all LDCs characterized by per capita incomes of between $100 and $200 per annum is 49 percent.[6] Since per capita income on Taiwan in 1952 was $179, its literacy rate did not, at that time, significantly distinguish it from similarly circumstanced LDCs. If one proceeds to consider the ratio of college educated individuals to the total population—even after the influx of relatively well-educated mainlanders—the educational level of the Taiwanese population at the time it commenced development did not distinguish it from populations in the average LDCs.[7] Clearly, the influx of

4. Cf. Philip J. Farley, Stephen S. Kaplan, and William H. Lewis, *Arms Across the Sea* (Washington, D.C.: Brookings Institution, 1978), pp. 10-11, Table 1-2.
5. Ian M. D. Little, "An Economic Reconnaissance," in *Economic Growth and Structural Change in Taiwan,* ed. Walter Galenson (Ithaca, N.Y.: Cornell University Press, 1979), p. 454; and Neil Jacoby, *U.S. Aid to Taiwan* (New York: Praeger, 1966).
6. Simon Kuznets, *Modern Economic Growth* (New Haven: Yale University Press, 1966), pp. 388-389, Table 7.4.
7. Henry Y. Wan, "Manpower, Industrialization and Export-led Growth—the Taiwan Experience," in *Growth, Distribution and Social Change: Essays on the Economy of the Republic of China,* ed. Yuan-li Wu and Kung-chia Yeh (Baltimore:

refugees after the debacle on the mainland was a manpower asset, replacing the drain of Japanese technicians and managerial personnel repatriated to Japan after the retrocession, but it clearly did not give Taiwan so much of an advantage as to make it a special case among developing LDCs.

An alternative explanation for Taiwan's special status among developing countries attributes special importance to the concessional aid afforded by the United States between 1950 and 1964—aid provided under particularly advantageous conditions. Often this is expressed vaguely in terms of Taiwan's "dependency" upon "heavy doses of foreign capital at critical times" without distinguishing between concessional aid and standard, non-concessional loans and investment.[8] Systematic American aid began in 1951 and continued through 1964. During this period U.S. economic aid amounted to $1.5 billion, averaging about $90 million per annum and $6 per capita. In the 1950s the level of aid—which reached about $10 per capita—was above the average received by other developing countries; but in the 1960s, when real growth began, there was no substantial difference. Taiwan was receiving $6.30 per capita against an average of $5.40 per capita for all developing countries. Some countries—i.e., South Vietnam, Zaire, Turkey, Yugoslavia, and Egypt—were receiving more aid per capita than was Taiwan. Many countries smaller than Taiwan received much more aid, particularly the French Overseas Departments and France's former colonies in Africa, as well as Cyprus, Israel, and Jordan.[9]

An instructive comparison is the amount of foreign aid provided Castro's Cuba by the socialist bloc nations of Eastern Europe. In a nine year period (1960-1969) about $2 billion in direct economic aid was provided.[10] In July 1970 Robert A. Hurwitch of the United States Department of State estimated that Cuba had received a total of about $3.2 billion in various forms of economic assistance from the Soviet Union from 1960 through 1970 at an estimated daily cost to the USSR of $1.4 million and an annual cost of $511 million.[11] Given its population of between seven and eight

University of Maryland School of Law, 1978), p. 157. There is little evidence to support Amsden's suggestion that after the Japanese occupation Taiwan had "one of the most literate populations among the underdeveloped countries." She does go on to admit that whatever the case Taiwan did not have the "trained manpower" required of industrialization. Amsden, "Taiwan's Economic History," p. 348.

8. Hill Gates, "Dependence and the Part-time Proletariat in Taiwan," *Modern China* 5, no. 3 (July 1979): 382.

9. Little, "An Economic Reconnaissance," pp. 457f.

10. Eric N. Baklanoff, "International Economic Relations," in *Revolutionary Change in Cuba*, ed. Carmelo Mesa-Lago (Pittsburgh: University of Pittsburgh Press, 1971), pp. 266-269.

11. U.S., Congress, House, *Cuba and the Caribbean, Hearings before the Subcommittee on Inter-American Affairs of the Committee on Foreign Affairs, House of Representatives*

million, the annual per capita aid received by Cuba was about $64—about six times higher than the per capita aid received by the population of Taiwan at the peak of United States aid. If the level of foreign economic aid were a *sufficient* condition for economic growth, it would be difficult to explain the stagnation of the Cuban economy. If the level of economic aid is the *necessary* condition for economic growth, then attention should be directed to intervening and contingent variables to explain the Taiwan phenomenon— since many other LDCs have received comparable economic aid and have not matched its record.

Most analysts are prepared to grant that U.S. aid to Taiwan was important in ensuring the political survival of the Republic of China in the hazardous environment that prevailed after the retreat from the mainland. But it is not at all clear that American aid was either necessary or essential to the economic development of Taiwan. In the mid-1950s American aid amounted to about 10 percent of Taiwan's gross domestic product—at a time when the island's defense burden was between 10 and 12 percent of GDP. Without American aid and without the inordinate defense burden, it would seem that Taiwan would have developed as rapidly—all other things being equal.[12] A considerable portion of U.S. aid was disbursed in terms of P.L. 480 agricultural surplus commodities—particularly wheat—largely employed to provide adequate levels of food supplies rather than directly to fuel development. P.L. 480 aid increased from $85.5 million during 1956-1960 to $262.5 million during 1961-1965 and was used in large part to supply the cereal requirements for the half million men under arms on Taiwan. Without the military requirement those men would have been released for productive labor and could have surely produced what they required. During the aid period more men were frozen into the military than were employed in the industrial and commercial sectors combined. Thus, the main function of U.S. aid during the 1950s and the first years of the 1960s was to sustain the government and maintain a suitable level of consumption until Taiwan could embark upon its growth.[13] During the 1950s and early 1960s it served the international political and strategic interests of the United States to underwrite the government on Taiwan and maintain its military forces. Without that assistance the Republic of China might not have survived.

In terms of our broader theoretical interest, therefore, there is no compelling reason to believe that Taiwan would not have developed without U.S. aid. There is even less reason to believe that American aid might fully explain the phenomenon of Taiwanese economic and industrial development.

(Washington, D.C.: Government Printing Office, 1970), p. 18.

12. Wan, "Manpower, Industrialization and Export-led Growth," pp. 156-157.

13. Cf. Keith Griffin, "An Assessment of Development in Taiwan," *World Development* 1, no. 6 (June 1973): 34.

This is not to say that some considerable part of U.S. aid was not well spent in capital formation and in infrastructural and educational investment. It only means that without the strategic and political constraints within which the Republic of China on Taiwan was forced to operate, the island, without concessional aid, could well have financed its development out of its own resources or through foreign, nonconcessional capital flows. [14]

More recently Herman Kahn has suggested that the development of Taiwan might be, in part, explained by the prevalence and persistance of the "Confucian ethic" among the people of the island. Kahn has argued that "societies based upon the Confucian ethic may in many ways be superior to the West in the pursuit of industrialization, affluence, and modernization"; [15] and since the Kuomintang of Taiwan systematically cultivates the Confucian ethic as part of official policy, the island's rapid development may constitute, as a consequence, a "special case." The Confucian ethic, after all, is endemic only to Asia.

For a variety of reasons Kahn's suggestion is interesting. First of all — and quite independent of our specific concerns — with Kahn's suggestion we have witnessed the transformation of what had been, at one time, part of the traditional wisdom of amateur sinologists: Confucianism, it was affirmed, was the ideology of reaction, and it inhibited China's march into the twentieth century. Now we are informed that Confucianism affords underdeveloped nations advantages denied to others not fortunate enough to be Confucian.

Sun Yat-sen, of course, had suggested something like that at the turn of the century. Sun, like Kahn in our own time, maintained that the traditional ethics of China inculcated an entire syndrome of personal and collective virtues conducive to the modernization and industrialization of China. [16] Like Sun, Kahn maintains that "a properly trained member of a Confucian culture will be hardworking, responsible, skillful, and (within the assigned or understood limits) ambitious and creative in helping the group (extended family, community, or company). There is much less emphasis [than in

---

14. Gustav Ranis, "Industrial Development," in *Economic Growth and Structural Change*, p. 253.

15. Herman Kahn, *World Economic Development 1979 and Beyond* (Boulder, Colo.: Westview Press, 1979), p. 121; cf. pp. 118-123; see also Little, "An Economic Reconnaissance," p. 461.

16. This is hardly the place to pursue the convoluted discussion that has developed about the "modernizing" or "reactionary" character of Confucianism. See, for example, Thomas A. Metzger, *Escape from Predicament: Neo-Confucianism and China's Evolving Political Culture* (New York: Columbia University Press, 1977) and the subsequent discussion in *Journal of Asian Studies* 39, no. 2 (February 1980): 237-290.

Western countries] on advancing individual (selfish) interests."[17] All of this is probably true in a suitably general sense. But no one to date has argued that Confucianism is either the necessary or sufficient condition for rapid modernization and industrialization. For his part, Kahn makes the appropriate disclaimer. He holds both South Korea and Taiwan as typifying "other developing nations in important ways" while noting that they might enjoy some indeterminate advantage because of their Confucian heritage.[18] The possession of a Confucian heritage might well constitute a contingent variable that serves as an "accelerator" of development in some unspecified measure, but it is difficult to appreciate how possession of the "Confucian ethic," in and of itself, could explain Taiwan's (or Japan's or South Korea's) rapid development or serve to render the Taiwan experience a "special case."[19]

All the remaining familiar arguments mustered to render the Taiwan case irrelevant in any assessment of development in the modern world—that industrialization in Taiwan remains superficial insofar as production is restricted almost exclusively to light manufacturing, or that industrialization on the island is nothing other than an extension of American and Japanese industry because the economy, for all practical purposes, is controlled by foreigners—merit little attention. As we have seen, industrial development on Taiwan has followed comparative advantage. Industrialization in Taiwan did begin with a rather narrow, light industrial base, but it has evolved over the years until now the economy shows considerable depth, maturity, and sophistication. Furthermore, the economy of Taiwan remains securely in the hands of the island Chinese. It is generally recognized that the basic constituents of the economy are in Taiwanese hands and significantly controlled, as we shall see, by the licensing procedures and the indicative and prescriptive legislation of the government of the Republic of China.[20]

That development in the Republic of China on Taiwan cannot be dismissed as a "special case" cannot be taken to mean, of course, that it can serve as a mimetic guide to development for remaining LDCs. No individual developmental experience can serve in such a capacity. Every developmental sequence is different in some respect. It is unlikely, for example, that developing nations will enjoy the global boom conditions of the 1950s and 1960s in the foreseeable future. Yet there is little doubt that those conditions contributed in significant measure to Taiwan's success. Furthermore, Taiwan's colonial experience, while not unique, was sufficiently different

17. Kahn, *World Economic Development,* p. 121.
18. Ibid., p. 333.
19. Amsden, "Taiwan's Economic History," p. 364; see Samir Amin, *Unequal Development,* (New York: Monthly Review, 1976), pp. 212-213.
20. See the discussion in Little, "An Economic Reconnaissance," pp. 478-479.

from that of many LDCs to make comparisons difficult. The Japanese, for example, were assiduous administrators and agricultural modernizers.[21] During their half century of occupation they contributed much to the infrastructural development of Taiwan—an infrastructural development that facilitated Taiwan's subsequent growth. But it must be remembered that Japan also contributed much to the industrial development of Korea, mostly in the North, and yet North Korea has not been notably successful in modernizing and industrializing. Similarly, the Castro revolution in Cuba inherited the finest transportation and infrastructural system in Latin America.[22] Agriculture had benefited from decades of North American modernization—and yet communist Cuba, in its twenty years of developmental efforts, has failed to record any significant agricultural, much less industrial, growth.

Finally, it would be unrealistic to advocate that all developing economies mimic Taiwan in adopting a policy of export-led growth. Limitations would quickly develop if any large number of LDCs simultaneously attempted to embark upon major export expansion programs involving labor-intensive industries. As Wan-son Tae recently observed, if all LDCs undertook to produce labor-intensive commodities for export, the terms of trade would rapidly render the enterprise futile.[23] Thus, it is most unlikely that in the future any significant collection of developing countries could match the export-led performance of Taiwan—or of South Korea, Singapore, or Hong Kong.

Whatever can be said of the Taiwanese achievement, it is unlikely that any developing nation could simply duplicate the Taiwanese experience. In some sense or another, in some part or another, each developmental experience will be "unique"—which is not to say that there is nothing to be learned from each.

It seems reasonably clear, for instance, that the role of the Kuomintang government in Taiwanese development has been of considerable, if indeterminate, significance. Samuel P. S. Ho has argued that the existence of a "strong government" committed to "economic development" constituted an undeniable asset in the successful development of Taiwan.[24] Americans who

---

21. See Ramon H. Myers, "Japanese Colonial Development Policy in Taiwan, 1865-1906: A Case of Bureaucratic Entrepreneurship," *Journal of Asian Studies* 22, no. 4 (August 1963): 433-449; and Ramon H. Myers and Adrienne Ching, "Agricultural Development in Taiwan Under Japanese Colonial Rule," ibid., 23, no. 4 (August 1964): 555-570.

22. See Daniel James, *Cuba: The First Soviet Satellite in the Americas* (New York: Avon, 1961), pp. 21-24; Lowry Nelson, *Cuba: The Measure of a Revolution* (Minneapolis: University of Minnesota Press, 1972), pp. 43-49.

23. Wan-son Tae, *Development of the Korean Economy* (Seoul: KDI Press, 1972), p. 58.

24. Samuel P. S. Ho, *Economic Development of Taiwan* (New Haven: Yale University

had to deal with Kuomintang officials during the years of U.S. aid have commented on the dispositions toward modernization and development that animated the Chinese on Taiwan,[25] and it seems clear that government policy has significantly influenced the direction and composition of Taiwanese economic activity. The Nationalists have employed land reform, food policy, foreign-exchange and import controls, bank credit allocation and interest rate policy, investment licensing, exchange entitlements, tax rebate conditions, control of the domestic terms of trade, profit repatriation policy on foreign investment, and the organization and function of farm, trade, industrial, research, and marketing associations as incentives and disincentives in fostering growth in conformity with the indicative plans put together by parastate agencies since the reorganization of government on Taiwan.[26] At every phase in the history of Taiwan's development the Nationalist government has exercised direct control or indirect influence.[27]

The control exercised by a "strong government" was at least in part a response to the injunctions of Sun Yat-sen. Furthermore, the insistence upon the rapid development of agriculture under conditions that would ensure income and welfare equity to rural producers as well as balanced agricultural and industrial growth reflected the thought of Sun. The emphasis on infrastructural articulation and development and the commitment to education were part of the min-sheng doctrines that made up the original economic policies of the Kuomintang. The exploitation of comparative advantage at various points in the cycle through which the industry on Taiwan would pass was also suggested in the writings of Sun. Finally, the readiness with which Taiwan accepted foreign concessional and nonconcessional aid and foreign loans and investment was a direct result of Sun's conception of international economic relations. Had Sun's antiimperialism entailed withdrawal from the international market economy, the development of Taiwan would have taken on far different characteristics. Thus, even after it was no longer necessary to appeal to the United States to underwrite Taiwan's foreign exchange deficits, the government on Taiwan welcomed foreign investment. As concessional aid ceased, private investment and foreign loans augmented capital formation on Taiwan. At present about $2 billion of Taiwan's foreign investment, half the total of foreign funds invested in the island's economy, originates in the United States.[28]

Press, 1978), p. 250.

25. Jacoby, *U.S. Aid to Taiwan,* pp. 225-226.

26. See Hung-chao Tai, "The Kuomintang and Modernization on Taiwan," in *Authoritarian Politics in Modern Society,* ed. Samuel P. Huntington and Clement H. Moore (New York: Basic Books, 1970), pp. 406-436.

27. See Amsden, "Taiwan's Economic History," pp. 355-363.

28. Republic of China, Council for Economic Planning and Development, *Taiwan Statistical Data Book* (Taipei: Council for Economic Planning and Development,

Even after "derecognition" by the United States, foreign investment continues to be high, and public foreign debts (loans to or guaranteed by the government) amount to $3.7 billion. The debt service ratio (a critical estimate of a nation's solvency) is about 6 percent, considerably lower than that of most borrowing nations.[29]

Foreign loans have been critical in the establishment of a number of major industries on Taiwan, including those involved in power generation, shipbuilding, and steel production. Without foreign nonconcessional loans and investment the development of Taiwan would have had an entirely different character and pace.

That the political authorities on Taiwan systematically sought foreign investment and foreign expertise in the development of the island reflects Sun Yat-sen's views on international economic cooperation. As we have seen, Sun insisted that China's development required foreign capital investment, the transfer of foreign technology, and the assistance of foreign expertise. A strong government, animated by a clear policy of balanced development involving the participation of international capital, guided growth and industrialization on Taiwan.

Over three decades Taiwan's economy, under the ministrations of an ideologically inspired government, registered an average annual growth rate of 7.3 percent throughout the 1950s and 9.1 percent throughout the 1960s. Because of the energy crisis and worldwide inflation in the 1970s, growth has been irregular; but the economy grew at 13.9 percent in 1978, and even in the midst of a world monetary and energy crisis in 1979 it registered a growth rate of 8.0 percent. All of this has taken place in an environment of remarkable stability—as well as impressive family income and welfare equity. A strong government, inspired by a reasonably clear programmatic guide to economic development and industrialization, has used international capital resources and skills to realize quite notable accomplishments.

The role of ideological commitments in all this becomes evident when one considers the strategies suggested by alternative ideological commitments. Among those alternative ideologies, neo-Marxist "dependency theory" occupies a prominent place. Had those responsible for economic development on Taiwan adopted the central theses of dependency theory they would have insisted, prior to any effort at industrialization, that the island significantly reduce or sever any ties to the international market economy. According to the central notions of dependency theory, any

June 1979), p. 238, Table 12-2.
29. C. C. Chang, "ROC Fiscal Policy and Development Financing," speech before the American Management Association International Seminar, November 5, 1979, Taipei, Taiwan.

involvement in the "capitalist" world economy would produce only "balance-of-payment difficulties, inflation, loss of national control of the industrializing process, slow economic growth or stagnation, [and] growing rigidity of social structure"[30] for any developing economy. According to dependency theorists, only nonparticipation in the international money economy would allow developing nations to experience self-sustaining rates of growth.[31]

According to dependency theorists, industrialization and economic growth are functions of the degree of noninvolvement in "international capitalist relations." Thus, had India not been "entangled" in a network of international capitalist relations, it "might have found in the course of time a shorter and surely less tortuous road toward a better and richer society."[32] Relations with advanced industrial nations retarded its industrial growth and development. According to this thesis, the more intimately the less developed country is drawn into the network of "capitalist" international trade, finance, and commerce, the more impaired its industrial development and economic growth.

According to the argument, those developing nations with only a few trading partners are the most vulnerable. This concentration allows one or two partners to monopolize the trade of the developing country. If the developing country concentrates on a restricted range of commodity production—generally agricultural or raw materials production—it becomes increasingly dependent.[33] Finally, because production in such circumstances almost invariably involves low-wage, labor-intensive techniques, the vast majority of the citizens of such a country find themselves sinking deeper and deeper into poverty. The net result is that the less developed country, once locked into relationship with the more advanced industrial countries, tends to lapse into a form of underdevelopment that is self-perpetuating and class-riven. The advanced countries, having the more diversified outlets and the more sophisticated and wider ranging methods of production, accompanied by higher wage rates, will show rapid economic growth, increasing technological innovation, and social harmony, while the less developed partner will stagnate or languish in negligible economic growth and suffer increasing

---

30. James D. Cockcroft, André Gunder Frank, and Dale L. Johnson, "Introduction" to *Dependence and Underdevelopment* (New York: Anchor Books, 1972), p. xii.
31. Frank, "The Development of Underdevelopment," in ibid., p. 11; and Pierre Jalée, *The Third World in World Economy* (New York: Monthly Review Press, 1969), p. 138.
32. Paul Baran, *The Political Economy of Growth* (New York: Monthly Review Press, 1957), p. 149; see Baran's comments on Japan, ibid., p. 158, n. 14.
33. See Johan Galtung, "A Structural Theory of Imperialism," *Journal of Peace Research* 13, no. 2 (1971): 52-87.

technological backwardness and social strife.[34]

Had the political authorities on Taiwan accepted such notions, the development of the island would have taken a significantly different course. Taiwan would have sought a "socialist breakthrough,"[35] a rupture of relations with the international capitalist market. It would have sought to nationalize its economy and institute a government-controlled prescriptive program of development. In effect, Taiwan, under the aegis of a strong government and the impetus of an alternative ideological commitment, would have embarked on a radically different program. The recent economic history of revolutionary Cuba suggests what such a program might have been like.

After 1959, possessed of as "strong" a government as that of Taiwan and just as animated by a strong desire to develop and industrialize the nation, Castro's Cuba embarked on its own program of economic growth. Like Taiwan, Cuba sought to industrialize its economy while providing income equity to its population. Cuba's circumstances at the commencement of its program of growth were remarkably like those of Taiwan in 1949. Revolutionary Cuba, like Taiwan, was an island economy characterized by labor-intensive primary goods production. Like Taiwan, Cuba was an island devoid of subsoil resources, with a relatively high population density, and with only a few trading partners. Like Taiwan, Cuba was situated about one hundred miles away from a threatening military giant.

The critical difference between the two turned on Cuba's commitment to some variant of dependency theory. Almost immediately, the Cuban revolutionary leadership undertook to rupture all ties with the international "capitalist" economic system. Entailed in that process was the creation of a "socialist" command economy with prescriptive planning governing the allocation of resources and capital commitments. The economy was no longer subject to open market constraints, and a radical redistribution of welfare alienated almost the entire commercial, professional, and entrepreneurial middle class. Mass education programs were initiated, and a systematic effort was undertaken to diversify agricultural production, expand the island's infrastructure, and rapidly develop the industrial sector.

What became immediately evident was the necessity of obtaining the capital resources required to fuel industrialization. Since the commitment to dependency theory precluded access to the international capital market, Cuba

34. See Samir Amin, *Accumulation on a World Scale* (New York: Monthly Review Press, 1974), "Afterword to the Second Edition."
35. See Susanne J. Bodenheimer, *The Ideology of Developmentalism: The American Paradigm-Surrogate for Latin American Studies* (Beverly Hills, Calif.: Sage Publications, 1971), p. 39.

sought economic aid and concessional loans from the socialist bloc. With such funds and capital goods transfers, Cuba's command economy embarked on the construction of factories according to a "general plan" of industrialization to the general neglect of agriculture.

By the mid-1960s it was evident that the effort to industrialize was a failure and that the national economy was sinking deeper and deeper into debt to the Eastern European socialist countries. An effort was made to restore economic equilibrium by retreating to "monocultural," but collectivized, agrarian pursuits: i.e., sugar production. All efforts notwithstanding, by 1969 Cuba failed to reach the levels of prerevolutionary sugar production. The goal of ten million tons for 1970 was unfulfilled by 15 percent. Although in that year Cuba finally managed to exceed the prerevolutionary sugar output record of 1952, that was accomplished only by borrowing sugar cane from the 1969 harvest and expanding the cropping period to one full year. Moreover, the 8.5 million tons harvested in 1970 required a serious reduction of practically all other productive activities. Since then growth in the nonagricultural sectors has probably been insignificant, to be compounded by an accumulated deficit in the balance of trade that by 1974 was already close to $5 billion (not counting the remittances for amortization of loans and payment of interest). According to Lowry Nelson, the effort of the Cuban revolutionaries to implement the policies implicit in what is now called dependency theory, together with incompetence unconstrained by market controls, "has been an almost unmitigated economic disaster."[36] For a small island without natural resources, the result has been economic stagnation, universal commodity rationing for its population, and international dependency of the nation on the largesse of the Soviet Union.[37]

The Republic of China on Taiwan avoided all this. From its very commencement, government policy was predicated on a conviction that international economic support could be obtained under conditions of mutual benefit and that with that support a mixed economy, governed by broad, indicative planning policies responsive to open market signals, could exploit comparative economic advantages to fuel a rate of economic growth that would transform the economy of Taiwan from one that was agricultural to one that was substantially modern (i.e., industrial) in character. In effect, economic development on Taiwan was mediated by political behaviors

---

36. Nelson, *Cuba: The Measure of a Revolution,* p. 196. See John E. Cooney, *Wall Street Journal,* December 16, 1974.

37. Carmelo Meso-Lago, "Economic Policies and Growth," in *Revolutionary Change in Cuba,* ed. Carmelo Meso-Lago, (Pittsburgh: University of Pittsburgh Press, 1971), p. 332. p. 332. Castro admitted as much in his speech before the First Cuban Communist Party Congress, December 1975; see *Granma* (Havana), January 4, 1976.

influenced by the convictions of Sun Yat-sen.

Indigenous political variables were of critical importance in the economic development of Taiwan. However much that development was influenced by American counsel—particularly during the early phases of growth—the responsiveness to such counsel was itself the consequence of notions about international political and economic relations worked out by Sun Yat-sen and the revolutionaries who collected around him during the first decades of the twentieth century.

Sun understood development to be the consequence of the interaction of foreign capital and technological support combined with national policies that would foster growth, savings, and equity. Sun advocated a policy of class collaboration within the nation, protection of private property as long as property enhanced the collective well-being, and international cooperation with those nations prepared to treat China with the requisite respect. By implication, Sun rejected every tenet of what is now identified as dependency theory.

Sun conceived involvement in international trade and commerce as being mutually beneficial to all parties under conditions of relative equality. Some of the principal agencies sustaining that trade and commerce were enterprises that could only be identified today as "multinationals." If the term "multinational" is understood to include all enterprises that operate in two or more countries, such enterprises have become critical in international capital exchanges and have influenced the development of all LDCs involved in the international market economy. Sun could hardly have anticipated the development of such international enterprises, but he must have had something like them in mind when he offered foreign capitalists joint-venture concessions in the China of his time. In any event, the role of such enterprises is now recognized as critical in the development of industrially retarded communities—and consequently they have come under increasing scrutiny.[38] Very often their effect on less developed economies has been characterized as "exploitative," reducing the ability of such economies to accumulate the capital necesssary to fuel economic and industrial development.[39] If such is in fact the case, Sun Yat-sen's strategy of development for

---

38. United Nations, *Multinational Corporations in World Development* (New York: United Nations Publications, 1974); U.S., Department of Commerce, *The Multinational Corporation—Studies on U.S. Foreign Investment* (New York: U.S. Department of Commerce, 1974), Vol. 1; Raymond Vernon, *Sovereignty at Bay—The Multinational Spread of U.S. Enterprises* (New York: Basic Books, 1971).

39. A. R. Neghandi and S. B. Prasad, *The Frightening Angels: A Study of U.S. Multinationals in Developing Nations* (Kent, Ohio: Kent State University Press, 1975); Arghiri Emmanuel, *Unequal Exchange: A Study of the Imperialism of Trade* (New York: Monthly Review Press, 1972); Susanne Bodenheimer, "Dependency and Imperialism: The Roots of Latin-American Underdevelopment," in *Readings in U.S.*

China, involving as it did massive capital inflows through just such agencies, would have been grievously dysfunctional, impairing any hope the Chinese may have had for their nation's development and industrialization.

In effect, much of the credibility of Sun's proposed strategy of development turns on an assessment of the effect of multinationals on the economic modernization of Taiwan. While there is little doubt that multinational enterprises have garnered impressive profits in undertakings on Taiwan, it it equally evident that the government of the Republic of China, influenced by the thought of Sun, has welcomed their activities and created an investment climate calculated to attract their participation in the developmental programs of the island. As a consequence, the investment climate for multinationals has been characterized as unique in the international investment community, and the authorities on Taiwan have insisted that such international enterprises have contributed positively to the economic and social development of Taiwan.[40]

To date, remarkably little work has been done on the influence of multinationals in the development of Taiwan,[41] even though it is well known that many multinational corporations have significant investments on the island. Ford, ITT, RCA, IBM, Union carbide, 3M, General Instrument, Zenith, Admiral, Goodyear, Singer, Gulf Oil, Pfizer, Parke Davis, Sylvania, Du Pont, Philips, Mitsubishi, Nippon Electric, Sumitomo Mitsui, Matsushita, Sanyo, Hitachi, and many others have established facilities in Taiwan. Most of the investment is concentrated in electronics, electronics assembly, and chemical and petrochemical enterprises. Foreign capital, for example, represents about 50 percent of all investment in the electronics industry. Of the twenty-two television manufacturers in Taiwan, over half are either owned by foreign nationals or were the consequence of joint-ventures or the result of cooperative agreements between Taiwanese and foreign corporations. Such companies produce about 80 percent of all television sets manufactured in Taiwan. As a consequence of this collaboration, the Republic of China has become the largest producer and exporter of television sets in Southeast Asia. In 1974 Taiwan produced over 2.5 million

Imperialism, ed. K. T. Fann and Donald C. Hodges (Boston: Porter Sargent, 1971); Theotonio dos Santos, "The Structure of Dependence," *American Economic Review* 60 (May 1970): 231-236. For a general discussion of dependency theory see Tony Smith, "The Underdevelopment of Development Literature," *World Politics* 31, no. 2 (January 1979): 247-288.

40. Industrial Development and Investment Center, *Foreign-Invested Enterprises in Taiwan, Republic of China* (Taipei: Industrial Development and Investment Center, 1972).

41. This has been acknowledged even by officials of the ROC government. Cf. *Free China Review,* November/December 1974, p. 34.

black and white television sets, of which 2.3 million were exported, mainly to the United States. Foreign capital is significant, if not predominant, in the chemical and pharmaceutical industries. Finally, of the top ten private productive enterprises of Taiwan in 1974, two were Japanese multinationals. More than half of the ten had entered into technical cooperation agreements with foreign multinationals. Of the more than 800 Taiwanese firms whose export volume exceeded $1 million in 1974, 210 were either joint-ventures or were owned by foreign nationals. Together they accounted for more than 40 percent of Taiwanese exports.[42]

In the effort to control the influence of foreign investors in the economic activities of the island, the government of the Republic of China licenses all foreign-owned subsidiaries and regulates all foreign investment through a parastate Investment Commission organized as a department of the Ministry of Economic Affairs. The Statute for Investment by Foreign Nationals (promulgated in July 1954) and the Statute for Technical Cooperation (promulgated in August 1962) provide the legal basis for such control and regulation. Under such statutes the Investment Commission passes on the suitability of foreign investment, the right to remit profits, equity capital, and royalties. After a foreign-invested enterprise is established, the commission continues to supervise its activities to prevent possible adverse effects resulting from unlicensed activities and lack of compliance with established practices. An effort is made to ensure that such investment produces technology transfers that can contribute to the economic development of the island.[43]

Furthermore, all foreign capital inflow, both loan and equity alike, must be approved by the Foreign Exchange Bureau of the national Central Bank. Similarly, all outflow of foreign exchange, whether in payment of interest, principal, or royalty, or for the importation of machinery, equipment, or merchandise, must be approved case by case. The remittance of capital on foreign investments may be made only after two years from the completion of the approved investment plan. After that interval, an investor may apply each year for foreign exchange in an amount equal to 20 percent of the total invested capital. Such constraints are applied to ensure that foreign investors may not simply invest in the island's economy to reap a

---

42. See *Taiwan Industrial Panorama* 3, no. 10 (October 1, 1975): 12; and China Credit Information Service, *Top 500: The Largest Industrial Corporations in the Republic of China 1979* (Taipei: China Credit Information Service, 1979).

43. In this regard, see S. E. Rolfe and Walter Damm, eds., *The Multinational Corporation in the World Economy—Direct Investment in Perspective* (New York: Praeger, 1972), pp. 121-130. For the laws governing foreign investment on Taiwan see *A Compilation of the Laws of.the Republic of China* (Taipei: David C. C. Kang, 1970), Vol. 3.

ready profit without contributing to its growth.

Beyond that a number of rather complex ownership regulations govern selected industries. Foreign equity ownership in basic metals manufacturing industries, for example, may not exceed 40 percent unless a case is specifically approved. Where wholly-owned subsidiaries are allowed, regulations govern export practices, and there may be requirements that a given percentage of equity ownership be transferred to Taiwanese investors within a specified period. Foreign investments in trust companies are limited to no more than 40 percent of the total shares of the company. In export-oriented foreign-owned or joint-venture enterprises, a local content requirement often accompanies licensing. The government directs that any such enterprise that processes or assembles goods for export use local supplies and suppliers, a requirement which fosters increased vertical integration of the production process and increases the portion of domestic value added to the final product. By 1974, for example, the local content requirements for refrigerators, black and white and color television sets, motorcycles, and automobiles were 90, 90, 70, 90, and 60 percent respectively. Recently, local content requirements have been increasing. The government also requires that a wholly-owned foreign subsidiary export a certain percentage of its products, thereby enhancing Taiwan's foreign exchange position. If the requirement is not met, the right to remit profit and interest may be suspended. United States subsidiaries in Taiwan have been very meticulous in meeting such requirements.[44]

There is, furthermore, a restriction on the scope of activities that can be undertaken by foreign-controlled or joint-venture enterprises. Such establishments are strictly forbidden, for instance, from undertaking business activities other than those approved by the Investment Commission. On the other hand, the government has been fostering mergers wherever such mergers might enhance competitive advantage and decrease production cost. Because much of Taiwan's economy remains burdened by many cost-inefficient small and medium-sized enterprises, foreign-owned companies are often encouraged to merge with local companies. Various kinds of tax incentives are used by different government agencies to effect such combinations—particularly in textile and other labor-intensive industries subject to severe competition from South Korea, Hong Kong, and Singapore. There is, moreover, some legislation governing industrial pollution. In January 1976 the government announced that any plant established with foreign capital would have to meet certain pollution restraint requirements.

---

44. See Ching-yuan Huang, *Multinationals in the Republic of China—Laws and Policies* (Taipei: Asia and the World Forum, October 1978), pp. 17-21.

Finally, because multinationals provide considerable employment in labor-intensive industries, there is considerable legislation governing job training through company-sponsored vocational programs. A statute enacted in 1972 requires that every enterprise employing more than forty persons allocate and deposit with a designated bank at least 1.5 percent of its total cash wage cost for use as an employee-training fund. Thus, in 1974 IBM provided $195,000 for training its employees to use new data processing technology, annually training sixty to seventy classes of students. Executives and middle-management personnel from other companies often take part in such courses and receive training in computer uses, teleprocessing, banking, and management. Such efforts add to the human capital on the island and offer upward mobility to members of the domestic labor force. The availability of such upward mobility has partially reversed the "brain drain" which for years drew off some of the best Taiwanese talent for more remunerative positions in the United States.

All this notwithstanding, it is obvious that the economic strength of multinationals, as well as Taiwan's dependence on their continued contribution to its economic well-being, make it difficult for the government to be aggressive in enforcing its passive and active legislative controls. Although it would not be accurate to characterize the relationship between multinationals and Taiwan as "exploitative" (since it would be unlikely that workers in Taiwan would enjoy higher salaries or better conditions under any other realistically conceivable arrangement), it is clear that the government must forever be cautious in its treatment of foreign investors.

It is clear that multinationals transfer their assembly operations to Taiwan to take advantage of its prevailing low labor costs (where wage rates are on the average about 10-15 percent of corresponding rates in the United States). The government is always in the unhappy position of attempting to maintain an "attractive" wage and labor relations environment for such enterprises out of fear of alienating them. Since multinationals establish plants on Taiwan specifically to enjoy low labor costs, any systematic effort to increase wages might well prompt the multinational enterprise simply to relocate where labor costs are more attractive. For a variety of reasons some multinationals have already stopped production on Taiwan or sold their plants. Bendix Corporation, Motorola, Televac, Philco-Ford, and Ampex are only a few of the multinational subsidiaries that either ceased operations on Taiwan or sold to other investors.

There is some evidence that multinationals, given the passivity of government agencies, have been less than diligent in protecting the health of their workers.[45] It appears, moreover, that multinationals are not rigorous in

---

45. Ibid., pp. 50-51.

meeting the requirements of Taiwan's Labor Union Law—in fact, most unions that do exist among multinationals give every appearance of being "company unions." In the past, when unions have been organized the employer has often selected the leadership. Supervisory personnel of the enterprise itself frequently are elected to union office, and the union is housed in the plant itself. Union officials are often given preferential employment and assigned preferred tasks. All of these practices strongly suggest employer domination.

Multinationals give every evidence of abetting, if not originating, such practices, and the government has not been in a position to offset them.[46] The only realistic way in which the interests of employees can be met under such conditions is by resolute government intervention—intervention that is becoming increasingly necessary, particularly when multinationals are involved. Whether such interventions will alienate some foreign investment is to be seen. The recent steady increase in wages prompted by labor scarcity has apparently not dampened foreign investment in Taiwan, which attained record levels in 1978 and 1979.[47]

Given these considerations, the involvement with multinational enterprises has been a mixed blessing for Taiwan. Their presence has created tensions and produced problems. There have been documented cases in which a multinational enterprise, seeking to evade the obligations imposed by law, has found the Foreign Exchange Bureau and the Ministry of Economic affairs resistant to its legal arguments and blandishments; but there have been many other instances in which the government of the Republic of China has made concessions to foreign establishments far in excess of anything required by equity or legal redress. The government has been largely concerned with maintaining a favorable investment climate on the island and characteristically has not employed its control instruments with the consistency and energy seemingly required. Multinational corporations on Taiwan continue to pursue compulsory purchase requirements with respect to their subsidiaries that, in fact, impair the Republic of China's trade balances. The government has done little to intervene, in part because of public passivity. Government measures, calculated to control labor relations, foreign exchange, truth in advertising, and pollution generation in the public

46. See U.S., Department of Labor, *Labor Law and Practice in the Republic of China (Taiwan)*, (Washington, D.C.: U.S. Government Printing Office, 1972).

47. Council for Economic Planning and Development, *A Brief Report on Taiwan's Economic Situation, 1978* (Taipei: Council for Economic Planning and Development, February 1979); Council for Economic Planning and Development, *A Brief Report on Taiwan's Economic Situation, 1979* (Taipei: Council for Economic Planning and Development, 1980); *China Post,* December 17, 1979; *Taiwan Statistical Data Book 1979*, p. 238, Table 12-2.

interest, have—by informed judgment—shown themselves to be ineffectively implemented or intrinsically inadequate. As a case in point, between 1976 and 1978 the Taiwan Provincial Water Pollution Prevention Agency inspected 1,493 factories and identified 1,079 that were not properly disposing of refuse water. By the end of 1978, only 251 had made the required improvements, 354 had been fined, and 828 continued with their offending practices. More sophisticated, informed, and effective legislation seems to be required.

Striking a balance between such control and maintaining an attractive investment climate is difficult. But government authorities on Taiwan are today in a much better bargaining position than they were fifteen years ago. National savings are now all but sufficient for financing new capital investment on Taiwan, considerably reducing the island's dependency on foreign investment. The labor force on Taiwan still constitutes one of the most attractive in Asia, and multinationals can expect to continue earning substantial returns by maintaining off-shore production there. Doubtless Taiwan will continue to remain an attractive arena for foreign capital investment without the government providing multinationals special advantage that might do disservice to Taiwan's overall program of enhanced social welfare.

The most important and durable contribution multinationals will make to Taiwan's future is the transfer of advanced technology. More than capital inflows, maturing Taiwan requires the sophisticated technology that only the United States, Japan, and Western Europe can provide. In this respect the Republic of China on Taiwan remains dependent, but it is a dependency that rational calculation can make mutually profitable without the hint or reality of exploitation.

It is reasonably clear that multinationals have enhanced, and can continue to enhance, the economic development of Taiwan. The activities of multinational corporations on Taiwan have certainly not contributed to, much less made inevitable, massive unemployment, impoverishment, or gross inequality.[48] Multinationals have assisted Taiwan in its export-led growth, provided jobs for its labor force, enhanced its industrial base, and improved its managerial skills. Capital inflow, employment opportunities, export generation, and tax remittances have all contributed to the economic development of Taiwan. Moreover, the multinationals have probably imparted important engineering, managerial, and technological skills without which long range, sustained growth could not have been achieved. During the 1950s and 1960s labor intensive technologies were welcomed and

48. See Richard J. Barnet and Ronald E. Muller, *Global Reach: The Power of Multinational Corporations* (New York: Simon and Schuster, 1974), p. 364; and Huang, *Multinationals,* pp. 178-179.

encouraged by legislative design. In the 1970s the government of the Republic of China has fostered the transfer of skill-intensive technology to service its drive to industrial maturity. Recently, the government has established the Industrial Research Institute to assist Taiwanese enterprise in acquiring and assimilating the advanced technology made available by multinational enterprises. Since the cost of such acquisition is high, and the short-run return is low, the involvement of parastate agencies has become a necessity. Given its stronger bargaining position and its more ample financial, and more abundant personnel, resources, the parastate agency can better serve as a vehicle for international technology transfer—and such a strategy may serve as a model by which developing countries can acquire advanced technology from multinational enterprises.

At the moment, technology transfers in the Republic of China are governed by legislation that allows for the capitalization of intangible assets by selling or licensing those assets. Once such assets are capitalized or licensed—an action required by the Investment Commission if the foreign investor seeks the benefits and protection provided by the laws of the Republic of China—the Statute for Technical Cooperation governs the relationship which results. In effect, technology is transferred with the capital investment of the foreign agent. The government acts as an interested party to any transaction between the foreign investor and the national enterprise. Depending on its bargaining leverage, the government will negotiate the best agreement possible for technology transfers.

By the mid-1970s foreign capital inflows contributed about 10 percent to the gross domestic capital formation of the economy, about 20 percent to the capital formation in industry in general, and more to those industries (like electronics) in which foreign capital became concentrated. Foreign investment, moreover, contributed to overall employment. By the mid-1970s about 13 percent of Taiwan's labor force was employed by foreign enterprises. Finally, foreign investment increased exports and helped the Republic of China acquire foreign exchange. The export earnings of the Taiwanese economy have clearly benefited from the marketing facilities of multinational enterprises, particularly in terms of off-shore purchasing. Without multinational investment, the foreign exchange gains could hardly have been realized.

The influence of multinationals on technological and skill transfers has been hard to estimate. There were 837 technical cooperation projects approved by the government of the Republic of China between foreign and indigenous companies between 1952 and 1974, but their precise effect has been hard to calculate. Clearly some of those backward and forward linkages to domestic industry—as well as some of the associated technological spinoffs—are only now being realized. The deepening of Taiwan's economy into more capital and skill-intensive undertakings would probably have been considerably more difficult without the technological, skill, and management transfers associated with foreign investment.[49]

In effect, there is little, if any, evidence that the multinationals in Taiwan have contributed to the making of a stagnant, no-growth economy. Nor does any evidence support the contention that foreign investment has succeeded in "decapitalizing" or "denationalizing" the Taiwanese economy. The multinationals have assisted the Taiwanese economy in its balance-of-payments position; and the repatriation of profits, facilitated by generous legislation, has not impaired the island's ability to proceed with impressive capital formation. When repatriated profits are compared with the magnitude of overall investment or with the volume of business generated in Taiwan, "decapitalization" through profit repatriation is revealed as a "radical" myth. In fact, the entire conception the the "imperialism" of developed countries must necessarily result in sectorally uneven and generally lower growth in real gross domestic product, with stagnant real wages and unfavorable terms of trade in the LDCs, appears to be similarly mythical.

This is not to say that multinational enterprises and advanced industrial states do not exercise significant, and perhaps preponderant, economic power vis-à-vis the LDCs—nor that any such power may not be employed to exploit underdeveloped communities. What it suggests is that any developing country that opens itself to foreign concessional or nonconcessional capital inflows must have a strong, autonomous state structure to insulate itself from exploitation—a state capable of controlling and directing foreign aid and investment in accordance with its own growth strategy. A strong state, in effect and as suggested by Sun Yat-sen, would be a prerequisite for equity in such a relationship.[50]

To maximize the benefits made available by foreign capital resources would, in turn, require that such a state could implement a growth strategy substantially independent of extranational influence as well as the interests of indigenous, traditional, landed upper classes and reactionary elites. Such a growth strategy might well restrict the special privileges of extranationals and encroach upon the property and status advantages of parochial interests—and the state would have to be shielded against their reaction. So much had been clear to Sun Yat-sen more than half a century ago. As circumstances would have it, the retreat of the Kuomintang from the mainland of China released it from the constraints imposed upon it by its mainland nonmovement allies and allowed it, unencumbered, to pursue the substance of Sun's

---

49. Ranis, "Industrial Development," p. 253; Huang, *Multinationals*, pp. 139-140.
50. Smith, "The Underdevelopment of Development Literature," pp. 277, 279, 280-281.

policies on Taiwan. What resulted was an autonomous state—characterized in the literature as "authoritarian"—possessed of a technically efficient, modernizing, and reasonably incorruptible bureaucracy neither recruited from nor responsible to traditional or privileged sectors of its underdeveloped community.[51] From that position of strength, the Kuomintang apparently could manage its relationship with the multinationals to Taiwan's general advantage.

In effect, the economic and industrial development of the Republic of China on Taiwan has been mediated by specifically political variables. Exogenous economic variables—including the relationship between itself and the developed, metropolitan countries—have not exclusively determined the outcome of its developmental efforts. The Republic of China on Taiwan has established that development can occur within the network of the world economy. It has established that underdevelopment is not generated by the very dynamics of "capitalism." Development can take place within international market relationships when the less developed country is possessed of a sufficiently strong, autonomous state apparatus that can effectively intervene to protect national interests in accordance with its own growth strategies.

Years ago Neil Jacoby suggested that "Taiwan will long stand as one of the signal successes of international economic cooperation in the postwar world. . . . Those peoples of other countries who aspire to make rapid progress would do well to study the record of Taiwan."[52] In a world in which the United States and the international market economy have very few successes to celebrate, the economic history of the Republic of China on Taiwan stands out as a compelling exception. In the long run, the success of Taiwan, won with capital, technological, military, and moral assistance from the nonsocialist economies, will probably count for more than any temporary defeats in the world arena.

More than that, the economic history of Taiwan suggests a great deal to those responsible for economic development in less developed countries. Since the political authorities on the Chinese mainland, for example, are now prepared to acknowledge the signal failures of Stalinist and Maoist economic strategies, the experience of Taiwan offers itself as an attractive alternative. Now that the communist authorities in mainland China have decided to enter into commercial and financial connection with the advanced nonsocialist nations of the West in their search for loans and joint-venture capital— and there is a general recognition of the need for more effective resource

---

51. See, for example, Ellen Kay Trimberger, *Revolution from Above: Military Bureaucrats and Developments in Japan, Turkey, Egypt, and Peru* (Edison, N.J.: Transaction Press, 1977).

52. Jacoby, *U.S. Aid to Taiwan,* p. 245.

and capital allocations, training, and management skills to absorb the more sophisticated technologies that are becoming more and more available — Beijing's apparent willingness to "learn from Taiwan" should perhaps include a reevaluation of Sun's ideas.

Now that the economic failures of mainland China have become apparent, the command economy model of economic development and industrialization has lost the unqualified appeal it had for more than a generation among the less developed nations. Correlative to that loss has been the increasing attractiveness of an alternative model best exemplified by the economic history of Taiwan. The substance of Taiwan's accomplishment is to be found in large part in the programmatic suggestions outlined in some of the earliest writings of Sun Yat-sen. Among other things, he saw economic development as a collaborative enterprise that involved intimate and extensive cooperation between the less developed and the advanced industrial states. Almost every other part of his proposed program is equally suggestive and merits consideration by those charged with the responsibility of guiding less developed countries through the stages of economic modernization and growth. For a generation events obscured the relevance of Sun's vision, but the advent of the 1980s seems to have placed them, once again, on the agenda—and Sun Yat-sen, an "antiimperialist" and "third world" theoretician, enjoys a significance in our own time that he perhaps never did in his own.[53]

---

53. See A. James Gregor and Maria Hsia Chang, "Marxism, Sun Yat-sen and the Concept of 'Imperialism,' " *Pacific Affairs* (in press).

INSTITUTE OF EAST ASIAN STUDIES PUBLICATIONS SERIES

China Research Monographs

1. James R. Townsend. *The Revolutionization of Chinese Youth: A Study of Chung-Kuo Ch'ing-nien,* 1967 ($3.00)

2. Richard Baum and Frederick C. Teiwes. *Ssu-Ch'ing: The Socialist Education Movement of 1962–1966,* 1968*

3. Robert Rinden and Roxane Witke. *The Red Flag Waves: A Guide to the Hung-ch'i p'iao-p'iao Collection,* 1968 ($4.50)

4. Klaus Mehnert. *Peking and the New Left: At Home and Abroad,* 1969*

5. George T. Yu. *China and Tanzania: A Study in Cooperative Interaction,* 1970

6. David D. Barrett. *Dixie Mission: The United States Army Observer Group in Yenam, 1944,* 1970 ($4.00)

7. John S. Service. *The Amerasia Papers: Some Problems in the History of US–China Relations,* 1971 ($4.00)

8. Daniel D. Lovelace. *China and "People's War" in Thailand, 1964–1969,* 1972*

9. Jonathan Porter. *Tseng Kuo-fan's Private Bureaucracy,* 1972 ($5.00)

10. Derek J. Waller. *The Kiangsi Soviet Republic: Mao and the National Congresses of 1931 and 1934,* 1973 ($5.00)

11. T. A. Bisson. *Yenan in June 1937: Talks with the Communist Leaders,* 1973 ($5.00)

12. Gordon Bennett. *Yundong: Mass Campaigns in Chinese Communist Leadership,* 1976 ($4.50)

sp. John B. Starr and Nancy A. Dyer. *Post-Liberation Works of Mao Zedong: A Bibliography and Index,* 1976 ($7.50)

13. Philip Huang, Lynda Bell, and Kathy Walker. *Chinese Communists and Rural Society, 1927–1934,* 1978 ($5.00)

14. Jeffrey G. Barlow. *Sun Yat-sen and the French, 1900–1908,* 1979 ($4.00)

15. Joyce K. Kallgren, Editor. *The People's Republic of China after Thirty Years: An Overview,* 1979 ($5.00)

16. Tong-eng Wang. *Economic Policies and Price Stability in China,* 1980 ($8.00)

17. Frederic Wakeman, Jr., Editor. *Ming and Qing Historical Studies in the People's Republic of China,* 1981 ($8.00)

18. Robert E. Bedeski. *State-Building in Modern China: The Kuomintang in the Prewar Period,* 1981 ($8.00)

19. Stanley Rosen. *The Role of Sent-Down Youth in the Chinese Cultural Revolution: The Case of Guangzhou,* 1981 ($8.00)

21. James Cole.*The People Versus the Taipings: Bao Lisheng's "Righteous Army of Dongan,"* 1981 ($6.00)

22. Dan C. Sanford. *The Future Association of Taiwan with the People's Republic of China,* 1982 ($8.00)

23. A. James Gregor with Maria Hsia Chang and Andrew B. Zimmerman. *Ideology and Development: Sun Yat-sen and the Economic History of Taiwan,* 1982 ($8.00)

---

*Out of print. May be ordered from University Microfilms, 300 North Zeeb Road, Ann Arbor, Michigan 48106.